OUR TIMELESS YEAR

ALSO BY BEVERLY ROBBINS (HAMILTON)

Grains of Sand

OUR TIMELESS YEAR

Miracles of Love Lighten the Clouds of Dementia

BEVERLY HAMILTON
AS INSPIRED BY ULF HAMILTON

COGENT PUBLISHING NY
PUTNAM VALLEY, NEW YORK

Published by Cogent Publishing NY
Imprint of The Whitson Group, Inc.
3 Miller Road, Putnam Valley, NY 10579
www.whitsongroup.com

Manufactured in the United States of America
First Edition

ISBN: 978-0-925776-18-1
1 2 3 4 5 6 7 — 17 16 15 14 13 12

*I dedicate this book to Ulf, who was my
greatest teacher during his most difficult times.
He taught me the value of the present
moment in an uncertain future.*

CONTENTS

Foreword xi

Preface...13

Introduction..15

PART I

1. Bev's Journey to Ulf...21

2. On the Road to Love 27

3. Family Time...33

4. Our Sedona Journey 44

5. The Journey Ends, the Now Begins...........................48

PART II

1. Being In the Present..53

2. "I Won't Forget God" 55

3. "God Listens When I Smile" 58

4. Oops, Wrong House...62

5. Melting the Masks..64

6. Exploring the Unknown..69

7. Ghosts of the Past..72

8. Discovering Self...75

9. Row, Row Your Boat 78

10. Fun at the Pharmacy..81

11. Back to the Red Rocks..84

12. Who am I?..89

13. I Don't Understand 92

14. Out to Sea 94

15. Christmas Time..96

16. It's About Time! 99

17. Play Time 104

18. Forgiveness..106

19. It's About Love 109

20. What is Death? 113

21. Letting Go of Anger..116

22. God Who?..119

23. Who Are YOU? 123

24. I Need Do Nothing 125

25. It Is Here, Now..128

26. Space Between the Dots 130

27. I AM Spirit 133

PART III

1. Life After "Life"..137

2. Beyond All Idols..140

3. Over the Rainbow 142

4. The Butterfly Way...144

5. Gifts from the Heart 146

6. Love Speaks...148

7. Behind the Clouds..150

8. The Light of Love...153

Epilogue..155

References 158

Addendum 159

OUR TIMELESS YEAR

Each small step will clear a little of the darkness away,
and understanding will finally come
to lighten every corner of the mind that has
been cleared of the debris that darkens it.
A Course in Miracles

Ulf Hamilton

FOREWORD

*T*his is a book whose time has come.

I first met Beverly Hamilton in 1974 when she sought me out because of her interest in working with children. At that time I was about to form what was to become the Center for Attitudinal Healing in Tiburon, California, whose purpose would be to help children with life threatening illnesses find inner peace. It is now a worldwide movement.

Beverly has a unique way of looking at the world, which she brings to her writings. With an upbeat attitude, she brings easy laughter into almost any situation. In 1975, after beating the odds of an early death from cancer, she shared with me her recently published book of poems, "Grains of Sand." The inspiring words of her poems greatly appealed to me, and I felt guided to introduce her to a newly published document of spiritual psychotherapy entitled "A Course in Miracles."

We stayed in touch as our lives expanded to include marriage partners who were also interested in spiritual paths. It was in that frame of mind that Beverly helped her husband, Ulf, cope with dementia.

Our Timeless Year tells the story of their last year together. It is a love story that will go to the center of everyone's heart. With candid honesty, transparency and authenticity it covers the highs and lows of this couple's journey.

As you read this book, ask yourself how you might feel and react towards your partner as his or her once known past slips away. What tools do you have that might help you discover a different way to communicate with each other? And what could you do to create a better quality of life for your loved one?

As Ulf's condition declined they both drew a great deal of strength from passages from *A Course in Miracles*, which are sprinkled throughout the book. These became their compass for navigating through many challenging times, with peace as their common goal. This led to many conversations in which Ulf made profound, yet simple, spiritual statements, which Beverly felt compelled to share with friends in a blog that I followed. Those writings became the basis for her book.

In *Our Timeless Year* Beverly shares, often with humor, how during this final journey with Ulf, she shifted her perception of their changing lives from fear to love, thereby finding a measure of quietness and peace in a time of sadness and loss.

Isn't that the miracle we all want?

GERALD JAMPOLSKY, MD

PREFACE

*A*fter graduating from a small college in Texas, my adventuresome spirit was open to new experiences. It was the late 50's and there weren't many options available for young women my age. When I accepted a position in an American school in Germany, I took my first steps alone into unknown territory.

The confidence I gained in my two years abroad led to more decisions that laid the foundation for both my outward and inner journey. Experience became my teacher. Learning to accept the unpredictable moments of life taught me to trust my inner guidance. It also helped prepare me for the moments I write about in this book.

It must have been my inner guidance that led me to Ulf because soon after we met it became apparent that we would be partners on this journey of discovery. Marriage taught us the value of sharing a common goal to learn and grow. We explored new ways to see the world differently through lessons learned from teachings such as those found in *A Course in Miracles*. Among many other things, the *Course* taught us the present is the only time there is, and the path to love, through forgiveness, releases us from our past and future. The spiritual teacher Eckhart Tolle shares similar thoughts in his book, *The Power of Now*, in which he says, "Make the NOW the primary focus of your life."

We had no idea how significant those words would be to us

until Ulf slowly entered his own "present moments" after he was diagnosed with dementia. A short time later, a diagnosis of sleep apnea was included, adding to my confusion. As I assimilated the emotional shock of this unexpected change in our lives, I took Ulf's hand and joined him in his new world. We faced many challenges and lessons as we explored this new territory. The most profound discovery we made on this perilous journey was if you don't expect fear to be waiting around every bend in the road, you find love instead... and a little laughter.

Ulf gradually began to forget events from his past and the relevance of time but he always remembered the teachings from the *Course* and Tolle about "being in the present moment." Therefore he felt he was growing spiritually, rather than regressing mentally. He would often say, "I'm not the person I used to be," and my ready reply was "Who is? And...who cares!" Then we would laugh.

Ulf, in his simple, uncomplicated way, guided us to another level of viewing the world without the benefit or burden of past or future, through the lens of love. I chronicled this new way of being with Ulf in a journal that allowed me to express the tenderness, tears and humor that defined our last year together. When Ulf's timeless journey was over, he joined with that universal love he called, "God."

After writing this journal, I revisited memories of our life together. While writing the stories of our past, I became aware of the gentle light of love guiding us along the path of our experience. This book is dedicated to opening our hearts to that love.

INTRODUCTION
The Diagnosis

*T*oday is our twenty third wedding anniversary and we have dinner reservations at our favorite restaurant. Little did I expect that I would be shedding silent tears on this festive occasion as Ulf sits next to me holding my hand. It has been seven years since our move from the San Francisco Bay Area to the mystical land of Sedona, Arizona. The lovely red rock vistas are suddenly shrouded in the mist that fills my eyes.

These tears come as the result of an appointment we had earlier today with a psychologist who had tested Ulf. He had initially gone to her for mild depression and she suggested the test. Nothing could have prepared me for the mind-numbing words she spoke to us: "I hope your affairs are in order because Ulf may have dementia."

Where do we go from here? How did we get here? In my mind there was no filing system for this information. I did not see this coming because its onset was so gradual. Between anxious breaths, my mind keeps searching for answers. At the same time, with much sadness, I am reminded of my many moments of frustration and impatience and how this must have confused Ulf.

Having worked professionally with hundreds of children who were labeled "less than perfect," I am familiar with our innate ability to mask weaknesses or disabilities. Unaware of the adaptive skills he was developing, Ulf had become masterful at the art of deflection. In spite of daily challenges he continued to present himself well, effectively handling his business responsibilities and relating well to the many friends in his life. When we are challenged in maintaining our normal everyday living pattern, it becomes difficult to discover the point where abilities cease and adaptation begins.

I knew very little about the diagnosis Ulf had been given, but something about it did not feel right. I was aware that an early diagnosis could deflect from the underlying cause. I sensed there was a missing piece to a very difficult puzzle and I wanted answers... or even a miracle. Those answers, however, did not come immediately. I became more keenly aware of signs in Ulf's behavior that pointed to what seemed to be an inevitable and scary destination.

Four months later Ulf began acting out his dreams by aggressively kicking in his sleep. When I would wake him up to ask what was happening, he would mumble, half asleep, "Some animal is trying to bite me!" We later learned he was not far from wrong: something was metaphorically biting him. The Internet was immediately helpful as I researched dreams and discovered that Ulf was acting out his dreams as a result of coming out of dream paralysis. Some sites suggested a connection to Obstructive Sleep Apnea, so I located an OSA site. I read that the common symptoms of sleep apnea are being overweight and snoring. This did not describe Ulf, who was lean and rarely snored. However, I did recall him occasionally gasping for breath while sleeping and he had daytime sleepiness. He also had mild depression. These symptoms pointed to the possibility that Ulf had sleep apnea. I also learned that a diagnosis could be made through a sleep study.

On an impulse and laced with some hope, I picked up the phone and called the University of Arizona to inquire if they had a sleep lab and was put in touch with the director of the unit. As fate would have it, the University was engaged in a study with Stanford

University on Sleep Apnea and Diminished Neurological Capacity. It was 2004, and this was the first major study linking these disorders. After a consultation, they accepted Ulf into their program and set up appointments for a sleep study and neurological testing. I have always known about synchronicity and how there are no mistakes in life, but something special was happening. We were in the right place at the right time. The diagnosis revealed that Ulf had significant sleep apnea (OSA), so he was given a CPAP machine that forced air into the lungs as he slept. Gradually, he responded to this treatment and his mental state gradually began to stabilize. We were cautiously optimistic and hoped this would solve Ulf's cognitive difficulties.

However, after a follow-up MRI, the other shoe dropped. The MRI scan revealed considerable damage to his brain due to chronic cerebral ischemic changes—silent strokes—over several years. This was caused by the nightly loss of oxygen Ulf had suffered as the result of his sleep apnea. My head was spinning as we were presented with yet another unfamiliar, devastating diagnosis.

After Ulf's diagnosis of OSA we were referred to Dr. Don Curran, a psychiatrist and sleep medicine specialist in our area. In our first meeting he told Ulf: "You can ease off the anti-depressants because you are now getting the proper treatment. Air!" He wrote later, "I enjoyed meeting Ulf and Beverly immediately. They were very bright, fun people to talk with. Ulf was receptive and willing to participate in any necessary changes. In my opinion, Ulf had been misdiagnosed with depression when sleep apnea was the culprit." He was right. No more depression.

A neurologist told us that Ulf's sleep apnea was the core cause of his dementia symptoms, a connection many doctors are still not making. The program Ulf participated in at the University of Arizona was among the first to do the research that led to making that connection. I was mystified when I first tried to grasp this connection, but looking back on it now, it only seems logical. After all, we are talking about deprivation of oxygen to the brain! What else would we expect when starving the organ that regulates the mind and body of its vital food every night? There is not a single living cell in our body that wouldn't react adversely to such abuse. Without oxygen, our brains die. Without oxygen we die. The sleep apnea treatment slowed Ulf's decline for several years, but the damage to his brain was irreversible.

Thanks to a *New York Times* article titled: Sleep Apnea Masking as Dementia, I contacted Dr. Steven Park, author of *Sleep Interrupted*. Dr. Park referred me to Dr. Mack Jones, author of *Deadly Sleep*. Both doctors submitted short segments which are included in the Appendix.

PART I

Be Open to Life and Live!

1. Bev's Journey to Ulf

The early sixties found me happily teaching children with special needs at an American school in Germany. The job provided ample vacation time for me to travel around Europe. Everything was a new adventure, eating escargot in Paris, singing beer-drinking songs at the Oktoberfest in Munich, skiing in Austria, riding a camel beside the Pyramids in Egypt and viewing the incredulous art of Italy. All this before I was twenty-five.

The fun and games came to a halt when I left two years later for Colorado, and enrolled at the University to study for my Master's degree. My goal was to learn more about children with special needs. Research on children with emotional and mental learning challenges was very limited at that time. My earlier experiences working with these children had taught me the importance of using laughter and positive feedback in their healing process. This approach was not in the University curriculum. Treating special needs children was a new field, and very little attention was given to these children except to bundle them into a "one size fits all" category, which I refused to do. I developed my own style. This approach to mental and emotional anomalies was to become a great resource to the challenges Ulf presented to me years later. After graduation I was hired by a treatment center for emotionally disturbed children near Denver.

It was the mid 60's and I was 28 years old. Without any prior symptoms, I doubled over in pain and was taken to the hospital. The doctors, thinking these were symptoms of a "hot" appendix, decided to rush in to fix it. To their surprise, they discovered a malignant tumor on my kidney instead. It seems the pain was the result of my body cutting off the blood supply to the tumor. The "cancer" label and all the bad news that went with it was imprinted on my forehead.

After surgery, the doctor, with my urgings for him to tell me the truth, said that if I lived through the next year, I might have a chance. And, if I lived, I should not have children. He was sympathetic and gentle as he delivered this sentence but it felt as if someone had just pulled a plug, deflating what little energy I had left after surgery. I had not expected the truth to be so devastating.

Three days prior to entering the hospital I had been in the ski resort of Vail, Colorado, with friends. Skiing was not my favorite sport so I begged off the Vail slopes to do some writing instead. I will never know what inspired me, but while sitting in an empty restaurant owned by a friend, I wrote "Death" on the page, and proceeded to write, or to take what felt like dictation. This, in part, is what I wrote that day:

Death says:
Smile on me. Be comfortable in my presence. Know
my form in life. Your rejection of me saddens, for your rejection is
Not of me, but life. Ask the questions of life in quest of me. Answer
These and step closer to my knowledge. Bring life into focus and
Befriend me. Only you do not acknowledge my name.
You have given me a name to shun, to fear. You have taken my gift and
Transformed me to represent the fears in the dark corners of
your ignorance. Broaden the scope of the mind's eye.
Extend it from the flowers to the stars.
Amid this spectrum is a crossing to Life, not Death.

Writing in this free-flowing format came naturally to me. For several years my curiosity about "what is this thing called life," had inspired me to write in essay form about subjects such as Love, Identity, Belief, Prejudice, Necessity of Doubt, etc. These thoughts about life eventually translated to a form similar to Haiku that became a small book, *Grains of Sand*, published ten years after my conversation with Death. The book's simple message tells how we are born into this reality, feel separated from our spirit, and become fearful. Then, when we are ready, we awaken to the love within each of us. The short version is—we come here looking for love, forgetting we *are* love.

Once I had befriended Death, my thoughts about the future following this diagnosis were somehow not so fearful. In fact the word "future" was erased from my mental handbook. I resigned myself to not having children, and perhaps not even getting married. Living for me was just one day at a time.

It was the summer of '67, a year and a half since my diagnosis, and I was still alive! As the possibility of living longer dawned on me, my adventurous spirit took over again. Throwing a few suitcases into the VW I had brought from Germany, I drove alone to San Francisco, a place I had never been, with three hundred dollars in my purse. Where to stay was not entered in my "what's next" playbook. Noticing a freeway sign about an hour from the city I remembered that a friend had moved there with her boyfriend. I stopped at the next gas station and called. (This was before cell phones.) She said, "Come on over. We're having a party." Needless to say, I rushed right over. It was a lovely afternoon gathering with live music and professional singles. After a while, one of the guests, a teacher, came up to me and said, "I understand you need a place to stay." She proceeded to give me the keys to her apartment for a week while she was on vacation. What a welcome to San Francisco!

By the end of that week, I was living in a large flat three blocks away, with four Pan Am stewardesses as roommates who were traveling most of the time. Soon after, I was hired for the best position in town for my specialty at a hospital child development clinic, also nearby. My job allowed me to be innovative and creative with the children I saw on a one-on-one basis. Each child taught me something about transformation of the spirit. Within a couple of months, I met a Norwegian man who gave parties for his friends aboard his schooner while sailing on the San Francisco Bay. I must have really taken to heart what Death said: "Be open to life and *Live!*"

My years in San Francisco were filled with friends, travel (such as beachcombing the South Pacific on my way to New Zealand), writing and just enjoying being alive. I shared a lovely flat with my friend Elaine. We loved entertaining friends, which often included someone playing folk songs on the guitar while we all sang. My friend Loren and I, both Pisces, began organizing Pisces parties every year. One was held at the Aquarium (after hours, of course), and several made it into the social column of the newspaper. During this period I began to consolidate my writings and asked a young artist in my Yoga class named Meillyn if she would put the words in calligraphy form. A year later, as an associate in an ad firm, she asked if she could put my words into book form. I naturally agreed. She wrapped my words into an exquisitely designed book, *Grains of Sand.*

My work at the clinic continued to be very satisfying and rewarding. Staying abreast of innovative studies regarding special needs children was essential. Attending classes in art therapy or seminars with Dr. Fritz Perls, founder of Gestalt Therapy, were stimulating and informative. My life included meditation retreats, reading the latest inspirational books and generally exploring my inner and outer life.

Part of that openness to explore new vistas led me to a lecture in the mid 70's by Dr. Ed Mitchell, physicist and astronaut. He was sharing the concepts of researching human potential and consciousness behind his newly formed Institute of Noetic Science (IONS). On further inquiry about IONS and because of my work with children, I was directed to Dr. Jerry Jampolsky, a psychiatrist. Jerry was in the process of forming the Center for Attitudinal Healing, a place for children with life-threatening illnesses and their families to visit and share their stories. I met with Jerry, who then introduced me to Judy Skutch who had just arrived from New York to participate in a research project at UC Medical Center on biofeedback and healing. I provided the subject for the project—a woman working at the clinic with me—who had been diagnosed with inoperable lung cancer, and Judy brought the healer, Dean Kraft. He must have been effective because I soon learned that the subject no longer had cancer. I also learned that Judy was on the board of Dr. Mitchell's institute. Following the threads of my curiosity has always led me to open doorways.

One of those doorways appeared in the fall of '75 when Jerry gave me a copy of a limited printing of a set of books that Judy had introduced to him titled *A Course in Miracles*. The *Course*, described as "a self-study curriculum that aims to assist its readers in achieving spiritual transformation," was scribed by Dr. Helen Schucman, and was a collaborative venture between Helen and Dr. William Thetford, two highly respected professors at Columbia University, who seemingly were unlikely candidates for this unusual mission. I also met their associate, Kenneth Wapnick, who had worked closely with Helen to formulate her writings into the three books that comprise *A Course in Miracles.* I learned that Helen had authorized Judy, through the Foundation for Inner Peace (www.acim.org), to publish the *Course.* Helen and Bill maintained that *A Course in Miracles* was not another religion but simply a "self-study set of books that expressed a universal spiritual theme." It emphasizes experience rather than theology. As one who learns from experience, this was a comfortable concept for me.

Looking back over the San Francisco years, my time there helped me grow in many unexpected ways. My greatest adventure, however, was still to come! Four years later, I met Ulf.

2. ON THE ROAD TO LOVE

*T*he bright fall colors of the grapevines matched my enthusiastic mood as I drove from the Napa Valley to San Francisco. I had started on another adventure, and was headed to my first business lunch. The year was 1979.

After years as an educator and therapist working with special needs children in hospitals, treatment centers and schools, I had just ventured into the business world. Encouraged by my New Zealand friends who suggested selling sheepskin products, I formed the Golden Fleece Sheepskin Company. I moved to Napa where there was a sheepskin tannery, and brought with me a formula developed in New Zealand for producing washable sheepskins. These sheepskins would prevent bedsores in immobilized patients, making them a very viable business product. VA hospitals around the country were my first clients. I was dedicated and excited about developing a successful business while learning something totally new and different.

My friend Loren had suggested I meet with a friend of his named Ulf Hamilton. Reason being that as an insurance broker with nursing home clients he might be a valuable connection. In a brief phone conversation with Ulf, we agreed to meet for lunch a few days later. So that he would recognize me, I told him I would be wearing a blue dress. When I arrived at the restaurant, a tall, handsome, charming gentleman approached me with a smile and said,

"I'm Ulf Hamilton. Are you Beverly?" Under those circumstances any woman he approached would have instantly said yes.

We were escorted to a table overlooking the San Francisco Bay. After years of lunching in the hospital cafeteria, I looked around and realized what I had been missing. Being in business certainly has its advantages! For Ulf, who specialized in medical insurance for cities, hospitals and businesses, this was a familiar setting for a working lunch.

As we settled at our table with a lovely view of the San Francisco Bay, we discussed my business and how his contacts could be helpful. After a while we began exchanging personal details, so I mentioned my work with children. Ulf told me that he had two children, eight and ten years old. With a touch of sadness in his voice he told me that he was separated from his wife and no longer living at home. Ignoring the boundaries of business lunch etiquette, of which I knew little, my counselor ears perked up and I asked, "Had you tried counseling?" In a voice mirroring his frustration, he said he had done whatever he could but nothing seemed to work. He added, "My main concern is for the children, so I'm with them as much as possible. I'm one of the coaches for my daughter's soccer team." I did not press the point but later learned that his wife's alcohol addiction was the core issue. Being the gentleman he was, he didn't mention this. Family was important to Ulf, so this decision to separate, made after years of struggling, was one that he had truly regretted having to make. Little did I know, while sitting and having my first business lunch with this stranger that we would be raising those children together!

It was over a month before I heard from Ulf about possible business clients. He asked if we could meet to discuss prices and procedures. When we met again, there was more sharing of personal stories as we began to feel comfortable with each other.

Since Ulf was from Sweden, I was curious as to why he had no accent or a Swedish last name. He told me that as a youngster he had been put in a boarding school on the East Coast, where his stepfather served as Swedish Consul General. Ulf later shared with me the history of his family. The large Hamilton Association in Sweden is the oldest family association of its kind within the House of Nobility. The original Hamilton, Hugo, came from Scotland and Ireland in the 1600's and received the rights of nobleman in the Swedish chamber of nobles and was given the title of count. My immediate question to Ulf was, "Does that mean *you* were born a count?" To which he replied with a smile, "Yes." Count Ulf! The family members I met later, including his father, were bright, unpretentious people, much like Ulf. His father and grandfather were both distinguished Naval Officers. What impressed me the most was the family genealogy, recorded in the Swedish House of Nobles, where photos and histories of family members dated back four centuries to the present.

For me, with great-grandparents who pioneered and homesteaded Wyoming, and grandparents who ventured to the island of Aruba, where I was born, this was something unheard of. My father's side of the family was more traceable, though not back to the 1600's! Our histories suggest that Ulf and I were an improbable match.

During our next lunch, our hands touched across the table as we hesitantly looked into each other's eyes. This led to a parting kiss. My feelings made me wonder what was happening. Our relationship was gradually shifting beyond the business boundary. The Golden Fleece Sheepskin Company just took a turn in the road as Ulf and I took our first cautious steps toward each other.

This turn was not on my road map. Much to my surprise, I learned that love has a way of creating its own path.

Ulf and Bev

I was attracted to Ulf's gentle and accepting nature that added a balance to my venturesome spirit, and after a while our times together became more frequent. This was a totally unexpected direction from my well thought-out plan to be a successful businesswoman, traveling the country. My life became a collage of business, falling in love with Ulf, and getting acquainted with his two children, Eric and Jenny.

For years, my curiosity invited thoughtful questions about life that I enjoyed writing and reading about. Books with spiritual themes filled my bookcase. Ulf noticed me reading *A Course in Miracles*, and began asking questions about how it might have an effect on someone's everyday life. Many discussions about the *Course's* teachings followed. Then one day Ulf said, "Let's talk more about the parts on forgiveness." As he read and practiced the *Course's* guidance, he began to see how helpful it could be in healing the wounds of his past relationships. We were both learning to look within, while sharing our private thoughts with each other. This sharing opened us to a greater capacity for love.

At this same time Ulf was also listening, while driving to see clients, to Wayne Dyer's early tapes on motivation that had been given to him by his office manager. Synchronicity again? Ulf seemed to be attracting these teachings that offered "another way" of viewing his experience.

Ulf soon met Judy and her husband, Bill (Whit) Whitson. He admired Whit's gentle, inquisitive nature and eclectic viewpoints and Judy's openness to whatever was happening. Whenever we were visiting with them, there was always laughter and great stories with a little wisdom thrown in.

Often when Ulf and I were together, walking or sitting across from each other at dinner, we would naturally discuss our uniquely diverse life situations. Both of us were in transition from the past we had known. Deep within me, I felt the comfort of being with Ulf. Perhaps it was his gentle voice in these sensitive interchanges. Our relationship became transfused with an unfamiliar energy that seemed like soft background music in the daily lives we led. This new way of connecting with another person touched both of us.

Everyone has stories that reflect the distortion of what we call love that are interlaced into our life script. Ulf shared his story with me. His mother, Margit, left him behind in Sweden when he was five to start a life in New York with her new husband. Ulf said he felt very alone looking out the window as boats went in and out of the harbor in Stockholm, thinking maybe his mother was on one of them. Over a year later, she brought him to America where he soon was sent off to boarding school. He was involved in many activities at school, such as being on the rowing team, but Margit rarely attended any school events, not even his graduation. Ulf was then sent back to Sweden to attend school there. He experienced very little family life while growing up.

When Margit's husband was assigned to the Swedish Consulate in San Francisco, they bought a large acreage in the Sonoma Valley and Ulf moved from Sweden to attend the University of California. After her husband died, Margit moved there and eventually developed a vineyard. Ulf assisted her in this venture and visited her often. She bought an airplane at age sixty and learned to fly. I saw in Margit a capable and independent person who seemed to be most comfortable when she was in control of a situation.

About a year and a half after seeing each other on a regular basis, Ulf and I decided to explore this new venture into "togetherness." We responded to an ad in the paper about a small Napa Valley estate. The new owners, who lived in Southern California, wanted to rent the property until they were ready to renovate. We lived there for two years. This house on a knoll overlooking vineyards in the Napa Valley, with a pool, hot tub, cabana, and incredible views, was a perfect setting for the beginning of my life with Ulf. Many discussions and decisions were made in the hot tub, at night, with a thousand stars listening and giving us the feeling that we were not alone. We liked being together. Nothing dramatic, just a natural connection that seemed "right." And inevitable!

3. FAMILY TIME

*U*lf and I took a close look at our feelings for each other. At our age there had been the usual disappointments in what we called love. Something else was occurring between us that did not fit our experiences. The qualities we admired in each other were the ones we wanted to explore within ourselves. Unknown to us at the time, we were embarking on a partnership in which each became the teacher to the other. Looking back, we both seemed to be following a silent inward map that would give us glimpses of a more expansive experience of love beyond our personal stories.

When Eric and Jenny were ten and twelve, they spent their summer vacation with us. Since Ulf was working during the day, it soon became clear to me that if I decided to continue the relationship with Ulf, it would include his children in a substantial way. It was also apparent to me that I would be carrying much of that responsibility. My professional experience with children gave me an insight into their need for boundaries, solid guidance, and a caring home.

Because of the children, marriage seemed to be an integral part of our path, so we began making plans to tie the knot. Two years after we met we were married in our garden, with flourishing grapevines and mountains with a waterfall as a backdrop. Eric was his father's best man and Jenny, my flower girl. She wrote a lovely poem that we included in the invitation. Many good friends and family surrounded us. Judy loaned me her dress and her grand-mother's necklace to wear on this special occasion. Bill Thetford did a reading from his book, *Choose Once Again,* selections from *A Course in Miracles.* Love, laughter and good cheer filled the air on this warm, sunny day as we embarked on our shared adventure.

Several months later, Eric and Jenny asked if they could come live with us. After the separation Ulf had continued to play a major role in their lives, taking them to the park every weekend for a pic-nic or rowing on the lake. They had a sound relationship with him and had also come to trust me. The decision of where they should live went to mediation. The mediators spoke with everyone con-cerned, and the children were directed by a judge to live with us, permanently and immediately.

When I first met Jenny, at age ten, she had lost her laughter and looked very sad. Eric's reaction to stress was to act out and get expelled from school. Despite that history, the children quickly adapted to the rules and structure we created in their new home. I responded to Eric's tantrums by saying, "That is not who you are," and the tantrums eventually subsided. Jenny kept her emotions in a tight grip. However, when the grip slipped, there was drama, which was often amusing, especially for Eric.

Both Eric and Jenny welcomed their new life with us. We began our family life in a lovely home with two relieved children, a very happy father, and me. Since I had already established a relationship with them, we settled into a normal routine. I said to the children, "You can call me Bev. You already have a mother. You are responsible for helping with chores and doing your laundry!" As with the chil-dren I had worked with, I brought a light touch and humor to their life. As they excelled in school and some laughter returned, it was clear that their perceptions of themselves were beginning to change.

Ulf and my mother, Evelyn, had a mutual fondness for each other. She brought her playfulness to our family, welcoming Eric and Jenny to her lake house in Wyoming for two summers. This is a home she had designed and built. She had them building rock walls, working in the garden and growing earthworms for fishing. My mother studied ballet as a young woman and later took courses in Greek Mythology. She also became a student of *A Course in Miracles*. My mother came to our home often and was always available to stay with the children, allowing Ulf and me time together, including trips to Sweden.

This is a sketch of my family history. My mother's parents, along with their two daughters, traveled to the island of Aruba from Wyoming in the early 30's to work for an oil company. Both daughters married while there. It was during the depression so my father sent much needed money home to his family in Texas. My grandfather, Robbie, whom I adored, wrote humorous poetry and played the banjo. My Grandma Josie created lush gardens and laughed a lot. It was an island paradise with a large American community. However, when I was six years old, we narrowly survived a German submarine attack on the island. Tracer bullets were flying by as we raced to bomb shelters while the men tried to shut down the oil refinery that was lit up like a Christmas tree, making it an easy target. We waited for the big boom, which miraculously didn't occur. My father asked me later, "Beverly, were you scared?" I said, "No. But I sure was shaking." Women and children were flown out two days later with fifty pounds allowed per family. I think it was at this time I lost any fascination with possessions.

The town in Texas we moved to had an abundance of children my age. We were very inventive in ways of expressing our youth, from hayrides to marching bands. It was a perfect environment for children to grow up in. My brother Jack and I also had cousins nearby. My cousin Charles and I were especially close. Charles, now a doctor, and his kind and energetic wife, Mary, embraced Ulf into their family with love and respect. We were included in many of their great, only-in-Texas celebrations of weddings—they have five children—holiday celebrations, parades, or any excuse to gather together. Ulf enjoyed the inclusiveness of these openhearted people. It gave him an experience of family that was unfamiliar to him. They expressed all the frailties and strengths of family life within a supportive framework, holding everyone's genuine interest at heart. As I said, there is nothing like family!

Margit, on the other hand, surprised me with an unexpected revelation. Ulf and I hosted her 75th birthday party that included many of her Swedish friends. After everyone had left, the two of us were alone, clearing the tables. Margit looked at me and for the first time ever, I saw tears in her eyes. She asked in a soft voice, "How can you love them?" With a quizzical look, I asked, "Love who?" She said, "The family." Startled, I said, "Margit you have a lovely family who love you." That was a sad moment. I felt incredible compassion for this woman who had just revealed to me her reluctance and inability to love.

Margit's emotional separateness speaks to all of us, making her a good teacher. We have all planted seeds of "I'm afraid to trust"… "I'm afraid to love," that bloom into our many masks, creating the illusion we are separate. When in reality, we are all connected through love.

After we had been married a couple of years, we moved closer to San Francisco lessening Ulf's commute. He had a prior contract with his company that allowed him to form his own corporation. It was a risk. However, because of Ulf's good and consistent service to his clients, they all followed him in his new venture. They trusted his efficient and consistent manner of handling their business and valued his integrity. These were the qualities Eric sought to emulate. This was an exciting time for us.

At some point, I became "Mom" to Ulf's children. This is something they were comfortable with and wanted to do. It also helped eliminate their peers asking, "Where is your 'real' mother?" This new role crept up on me and felt so natural. Gradually I embraced the emotional impact of becoming this "mom" person. Because of an earlier medical diagnosis, I never thought I would live to be married and be raising two children.

Our family discussions revolved around the children's school activities, current events, exploring a new idea or how the day went for everyone. We also had discussions on the effects of a parent's addiction on children. This was an emerging field of study. Hugs were frequent as were expressions of "I love you" that were spoken often and written in lovely poems. I became aware of an energetic bonding among the four of us when we were together.

Eric began writing his own science fiction stories and preformed in school plays. One Christmas, to our surprise, he chose a set of Shakespeare's writings instead of a bicycle. He also played on the water polo team. We have a photo of him beaming while proudly wearing three winner's medals in the Academic Decathlon competition with other schools. For a kid who had been booted out of the second grade, this was quite an accomplishment. Jenny, who was always near the head of her class, belonged to several school organizations and enjoyed writing. She became editor of the high school Literary Magazine.

Over the years, our home was full of friends sharing stories, laughter, and our friend, Jim Bolen, playing the guitar. Previously,

I had volunteered at his *New Realities* magazine, which contained many articles that interested us, including the first article on *A Course in Miracles* with a picture of Judy on the cover. He also knew and interviewed Richard Bach. *Jonathan Livingston Seagull* is still on my bookshelf. Ron Hawke, a research scientist, and his wife Nancy, who also played guitar and sang songs she wrote, were raising five "his and her" children. You can imagine how we regaled each other telling kid stories. There is nothing like good friends sharing similar experiences with common goals for your children.

A few of Ulf's classmates in Sweden became lifelong friends. On several occasions we hosted them here and in turn were welcome guests in their homes in Sweden. Ulf and I attended his 50th reunion at his school in Sweden. We also exchanged visits with a good friend Henrik, who he served with in the Swedish Army, and his wife, Didi. Ulf said the most difficult part of being in the army was convincing a Swedish farmer to lend his tractor to pull a cannon!

Maintaining these Swedish connections, including those in the Bay Area, was very significant to Ulf. On our trips to Sweden, we visited with Ulf's father, Percy, and his stepmother, Ulrika. Ulf was very fond of this kind and enterprising woman who had a long and loving relationship with his father.

Both Eric and Jenny vacationed in Sweden, staying with Ulf's classmates. Eric even attended a Swedish school for several months. This gave him the opportunity to spend time with his grandfather. After graduation, Jenny was invited to spend the summer with another of Ulf's classmates, who had a daughter Jenny's age who had previously visited our home.

Being around these congenial, extended family friends had a positive effect on Eric and Jenny. Ulf and I were establishing a solid foundation for the children to expand and learn to like themselves again. With this added confidence in their abilities, they were later accepted into the University of California. As we were praising ourselves for having come this far, there came an unexpected change in the family dynamics.

When Jenny was just seventeen, and in that vulnerable transition stage, her grandmother Margit promised the ranch to her, and later to Eric, excluding their father. Information regarding the ranch and vineyard business was not shared with their father. It was the beginning of their team. Along with Jenny's immaturity and burgeoning independence, this promise gave her a sense of entitlement that resulted in some very poor decision-making. Just what parents need!

Nothing usually surprised me with Margit. However, one day in front of Eric and me, Margit said to Ulf, "If you come with Eric to the ranch, I'll call the sheriff"—her favorite ally. Puzzled and exasperated I asked, "What are you doing to your family?" Margit responded very curtly, "Anything I want!" She was right. She had something Eric and Jenny wanted, so they fell into line. Over the years they formed a business partnership and served each other well. We continued to maintain a relationship with Margit but the subtle line in the sand was always there.

Ulf had no objection to her decision. In fact, we had family discussions about not having expectations of inheritance. It was her right to give it to whomever she wished—even the sheriff! But Margit's untimely act and the underlying intent to keep him separate from this family endeavor was distressing for Ulf. However, this served the good purpose of putting Ulf on the path to healing his relationship with his mother. Exaggerations are good teachers!

Ulf's journey to value his inner strength, which requires courage and willingness, seems to have been his life's purpose. These words in Ulf's letters to Eric speak so clearly to his desire to learn from his family experience and to share his insights with his son:

> Dear Eric,
>
> So much has happened since you left! Bev and I have had a wonderful time together. Margit has not changed, as expected, but my feelings toward her have. I have released my anger and resentment. She is a Spirit and joined with the Universe just as are you, Jenny, Bev, and myself. It is a peaceful frame of the world I see. My lesson in the Course today is "Miracles are seen in light, and light and strength are one."
> Love, Dad

> Dear Eric,
>
> I empathize with your feelings about the family. I certainly understand, since this situation has distressed me greatly. Margit had made it clear that I am not welcome in her family configuration and I rarely hear from Jenny. This exclusion is not new to me. So now the challenge is to transform the energy and see it differently.
>
> The real lesson is we only attack ourselves and have this mirrored back to us. How wonderful the wisdom of hindsight is! All that matters is forgiveness and the past dissolves in the midst of incorrect perception. The important part of all this is to have respect for yourself.
>
> I feel privileged to have the opportunity to re-establish our relationship in the frame of our spirit selves. This is the true expression of love as I see it. We come to each other with a full cup to share our equality with full openness.
>
> Let me tell you, wherever you are, I am there in spirit! You are a searcher and you must continue seeking until you find it within. The answer lies there waiting for you to accept it and love it. How you see your truth is your

personal experience. The connection to the Universal energy is in your heart and it only hears and moves with your connected feelings.

Love, Your Dad

Dear Dad,

Ever since we started writing to each other, I just sit down and start with whatever comes up. I know you don't mind and you will answer my thoughts with your own. You do realize how happy that makes me feel, don't you? You are open and strong in your thoughts, flexible in your mind, and careful in your considerations

As to my mandate, I am studying Japanese, Buddhism and Energy. The Course is helpful in the last one. I am also writing. It's fun because writing is a way of reaffirming my own ideas about my world....

Write to me what you think of what I've written. I am so proud to have you as my father.

Your son, Eric

Communication lessened as Eric and Jenny became more involved with their personal goals concerning the ranch.

Eric and Jenny's life took divergent paths. While at the university, Eric studied Japanese and taught visiting Japanese students English. His interest in Japanese culture and language, translated into him flying to Japan directly after graduation where he was hired to teach English. His language and technical skills later qualified him for a job in Japan with Apple Computer. He married a lovely woman, Yoriko, and they have a precious and lively little daughter, Marissa. They live in Tokyo where Eric now has his own consulting firm that serves several countries.

Jenny's job as a graphic designer at the university newspaper that had a large daily circulation influenced her to make graphic design her career. She married Randy, a loving man with creative talent in the communications field. They have three bright and enthusiastic young children. Besides caring for the children, Jenny also raises goats, chickens, and rabbits, and grows vegetables. She is passionate about the environment and eating locally farmed foods.

After Eric and Jenny became independent, they re-established their relationship with their mother. They continued to partner with Margit in managing the vineyard, and Jenny assumed the role of overseeing the care for both women. With Margit in capable hands, Ulf and I decided to move to our lovely vacation rental home on a small golf course in Sedona with magnificent red rock views. It opened yet another chapter in our life together.

In her later years, Margit began to mellow. Ulf and I regularly traveled to California for business and to check in on her. On one of our visits, we located an exceptional caregiver, Loata , making it possible for Margit to remain on her ranch where we often stayed. Loata and I frequently scoured Goodwill collecting items for her village in Fiji where she had been a Math teacher. She was the perfect caregiver for Margit, who had fired many predecessors. One day while Ulf and I were staying at the ranch Ulf asked Margit if she would like a glass of wine before dinner. Margit said, "No, a ship just arrived and when the people get here, I'll have to call the sheriff. I don't want him to think I've been drinking." I thought, umm, this could be interesting. Nothing happened, at least that I could see. The next day when we told Loata this story, she said, "Oh my! The man my husband takes care of in the next town said the same thing at the same time. Only his guy wanted him to prepare for a party!" We all had a hearty laugh. They were both having the same vision, except Margit was going to call the sheriff and the other person wanted to throw a party. Margit provided lots of chuckles for us. Loata also saw people the rest of us can't see. The day after Margit died, she said she saw her sitting in a chair. I asked Loata if she said anything. "Yes. Margit told me in a very stern voice, 'Tell them I'm not dead!'" Loata added with a smile that Margit had told her on several occasions, "When your dead, your dead!" We all had a good laugh.

Family stories are filled with many opportunities to practice forgiveness. If we keep turning our kaleidoscope, we learn, as Ulf did, we are not our stories but the light of love that shines through them.

4. Our Sedona Journey

*S*edona promised a totally new adventure for us. Our condo was situated in a small country club environment. Our garden and pond bordered on an executive golf course with incredible views of the magnificent red rock formations.

Ulf and I first discovered Sedona in 1987 through a friend of ours who suggested we visit there, calling it a beautiful mystical place. Something in me was touched by the possibility of experiencing it, and Ulf, equally intrigued said, "Let's go!"

As we approached Sedona a picturesque landscape of dramatic red rock sculptures emerged from an evergreen background under a brilliant blue sky. What an amazing sight. I felt as if our life was about to change. We drove around the scenic area, hiked some of the many trails, visited the art galleries, and often sat quietly on Bell Rock, breathing in the beauty. Ulf resonates with nature and felt very much at home surrounded by this unique expression of its splendor. So it's probably not surprising that when we happened upon a small golf club development and saw a realtor's open house, we had a look around. Before leaving, we put down a refundable deposit. On the flight home we asked each other, "What did we just do?" We agreed we could back out of it, but never did and never regretted it. Not only was it a good vacation rental investment, it became a retreat for us and many of our friends, until we moved there nine years later.

The day before we moved to Sedona permanently, Judy and Whit invited us, along with other friends, to their home to meet Dr. John Mack, a Pulitzer Prize winning writer and Professor of Psychiatry at Harvard. His primary interest was in exploring the frontiers of human experience to transform individual consciousness. He had recently written a book, *Alien Abduction*. His research team investigated and recorded incidences around the world where people had witnessed UFO sightings and made personal contact. He showed a video of interviewing children who had this experience. Their statements were profoundly believable. It was an intriguing subject that made me wonder why it's so maligned and trivialized. The next day we were on the road to our new home. It was Ulf's birthday!

A week after our arrival, Judy contacted us and asked if we would sponsor a seminar for Dr. Mack. Although we had never produced a seminar, we agreed. For a start, Ulf and I went to the Unity Church and asked the minister, Max Lafser, if he would post a flyer of the event on their bulletin board. When we learned that he and his wife, Rama, also knew Judy and Whit, the meeting seemed destined to happen. Judy does have a way of connecting people.

Ulf and I attended services at the Unity Church. Max impressed us with his thoughtful insights and his easy, simple presentation. Ulf admired his unassuming manner and we maintained our friendship over the years. We learned Max and Rama had created a program in Conflict Resolution that took them to many of the provinces in the Soviet Union plus Ireland, Israel and Palestine. It was such a pleasure to share this part of our journey with these giving and light-hearted people. Ulf considered Max one of his kindliest friends, and the feeling was mutual.

With the help of the Internet Ulf was able to conduct business both in California, where we traveled to frequently, and in Arizona where he was involved with the business community. We lived in a congenial community with a clubhouse where many parties and events took place. Most of our neighbors had retired there from various parts of the country, making for a diverse community. When Ulf and I played golf on our small course, whoever lost fewer golf balls won. The great outdoors with its many trails was minutes away. We had lively dinner parties with an array of interesting guests who entertained us with their many stories. One of those guests was John Soderberg, who shared Ulf's Swedish heritage. He is an incredible bronze sculptor of historic figures, many residing in the Crystal Cathedral Sculptor Garden in Los Angeles. *Moses Coming Down from the Mountain* is my favorite. With this array of activities and friendships, there was nothing lacking in our life.

That is until Ulf's diagnosis in 2004 caught us totally off guard. Even though his treatment initially seemed to be effective, our life slowly began to change. We maintained our social life, but I was always alert to changes in him. Ulf and I spoke often about these changes. We even enrolled in a seminar teaching the Sedona Method, a simple process of releasing emotions that was very helpful to Ulf in dealing with the feelings of anger and frustration that accompanied the changes to his cognition.

My best times occurred when I was being creative. While I continued to research the apnea/dementia connection, my friend, Kathleen, who had been a documentary filmmaker, suggested I attend a Digital Short Story film class. This gave me the opportunity to chronicle a ten minute video on DVD titled "Sleeping to Death," Ulf's path of apnea masked as dementia. Ulf was superb as an actor portraying himself! My second five minute DVD, "How the Step Fell Out of Stepmother," can be seen on YouTube. These projects were a welcome distraction for me.

Then, two years later in 2007, Ulf and I met our friend Dan for lunch. Dan told us of his newest venture to create an Internet Radio show with his friend Linda, who had worked with him in Silicon Valley. Intrigued, I asked, "What are you waiting for?" He replied, "A first host." He then looked at me, brightened up and said, "Beverly, why don't you do it?" Ulf smiled and said, "I think you're on to something, Dan." The first Sedona Talk Radio Internet show was launched then and there. My show was titled: "*A Course in Miracles and Other Fun Things.*" My first guests were Jerry Jampolsky and his wife Diane, who soon had their own show sharing information and connecting with their Centers for Attitudinal Healing around the world. Doing this show gave me another opportunity to create something fresh and new in my uncertain life.

Ulf had his own creative moments. He wrote this message to himself and taped it on the wall by his computer:

MY CHALLENGES WITH
MY BRAIN
ARE A NEW AND
CREATIVE CONTRACT
BETWEEN ME AND GOD
TO TEACH ME TO LAUGH
AT THE CHILDISHNESS
OF WHAT I HAVE INVENTED
TO BLOCK LOVE

5. THE JOURNEY ENDS, THE NOW BEGINS

*W*ith Ulf's diagnosis of dementia and sleep apnea five years earlier, we were well launched on our new path. He stabilized for several years and always tended to his personal care. In the event I became unable to care for Ulf, we returned to Northern California where Jenny and her family lived. The long process of selling our home and moving was stressful for both of us. Fortunately, we moved to a lovely community in the Sonoma Wine Country, with expansive views of the mountains overlooking the golf course. This setting had a calming effect on both of us.

The re-circuiting of Ulf's brain altered his experience as his perception of himself shifted. He slowly began to accept what was happening to him. As I started listening closely to Ulf, I became aware that something, uncommon to me, was taking place. These touching moments would have ended up in a jumble of fragmented memories had I not written them down as they occurred.

The guidance to write down Ulf's new way of viewing his world came to me from angels and Linda Patrick. We had met Linda at one of Dan's musical Karaoke gatherings in Sedona. Like us, she had also recently moved to Northern California from Sedona. She called and suggested getting together, so I invited her to lunch at our place. While enjoying our meal on the patio, Ulf spoke of the aliveness of nature by telling us to notice how the breeze moves the trees. His normal sensitivity to nature had become amplified. His words captured our attention with simple statements like "There is no time where God is."

After a while Linda, a skilled computer tech said, "Beverly, you need to record this." I asked, "How?" We went directly to the computer and she set up the format, saying, "Now all you have to do is write." When we returned to the patio, she said, "Do you know I talk to angels?" I knew little about her but to open one's heart to touch an angel is endearing. She said, "My angels have been urging me to call you but I ignored them, yet they kept on insisting, so I called." After the first weeks of writing that I shared with others over the Internet, I more fully appreciated the loving gift wrapped in her message. The following chapters are the result of that writing.

Our new home environment is perfect for us. Not knowing anyone nearby, the quiet solitude resembles a retreat, giving Ulf comfort in relaxing his defenses and just being who he is. These interactions and thoughts were written in this peaceful setting.

Ulf's final year brought laughter, tears and a new way of looking at our relationship. I entered Ulf's new world and did what any loving partner would do. I took his hand as we stepped toward this unknown horizon. At a time that could be described as very difficult, we experienced some of the most precious moments of our life together. He was my teacher and still is!

PART II

Love is Always Right Now

<small>ULF WROTE THIS TO ME ON OUR 20TH ANNIVERSARY</small>

Letter to My Wife

There was a time when you and I were play-mates. We still are but with a difference. I found in you a soul mate like no other in my life. You brought awareness to me, excitement of the spirit, direction to my children and the opportunity to grow with the love of my life.

In the years we have shared you have guided me to look within. You have brought to me an understanding of what it means to give. I am still working on this one! You have opened the door to love, not of this world, but of oneness. You are as much a part of me as breathing. As we grow, I know that we more fully will experience love through our evolving awareness and openness to universal guidance.

Now it is my turn to guide! (And guide he did!)

Let's be in the experience every moment!

Your loving husband, Ulf

1. Being In the Present

*A*s Ulf slowly began to lose his memory of past events and all sense of time, it became obvious to me that the way we had related in the past was going to change significantly. I needed to decide whether to hang on to something that no longer existed for him or to go where he is "now."

We are living in a peaceful environment with very comfortable chairs and a mountain view that invites our morning readings and welcomes the quieting of our mind. Ulf often reads Eckhart Tolle's books such as *Power of Now*, or his Weekly Reminders, which I print out for him. Ulf relates to his simple way of using few words to express spiritual thoughts. Today he looks up from his reading and asks if he can share something with me. I nod affirmatively and say, "Sure, I'd love to hear it." Ulf begins reading aloud from Tolle's newsletter:

> "To be free of thousands of years of conditioning does not require time or future. At this moment you can step out of the movement of thought and allow quite simply an alert presence to be there."

We sit quietly musing on these thoughts. I then ask Ulf, "What do these words say to you?" He quickly replies, "I guess it's all right for me to forget." I laugh and say, "Hey, maybe you're on the road to enlightenment!

Part of my challenge in sharing Ulf's "being in the present" is to shift my own perception of the importance I place on the past with regard to our relationship. One day Ulf looks up at me from his chair and asks hesitantly, "We are married, aren't we?" Holding my breath, my first thought was, "I'm not ready for this." I slowly exhaled and said, "We sure are and you are a wonderful husband." That seemed to please him. I was aware that parts of his past were no longer present, but this was very personal for me. I subsequently realized that there is much of our shared past that he no longer remembers. It is a riveting experience for me to realize that my husband has lost an aspect that most couples regard as essential to the bond we call love. I am becoming increasingly aware, when I'm reminded of some memory, that I can rarely share this common experience. This is going to require some altering of my beliefs as to what has value in our relationship. He does remember family and good friends, just not the details of the story.

My conscious attempt to minimize our personal history and focus on being in the present brings me a hint of recognition of what Ulf is experiencing. This getting into the "Present Moment" is a grieving and mourning passage of what I thought was "real" in our relationship. It is what gave sustenance and meaning to my life. I am increasingly aware of my attachment to the "past." Words I had read and embraced for years are now figures in a nightmare demanding that I face "reality." "Letting go" and "giving up the past" have become daily reminders of loss as Ulf and I face each day. I have a choice: to suffer attachment to our past or to surrender that attachment and join Ulf in his present moment. Choosing to surrender my expectations and share the present with Ulf requires that our book of life together have only one page, one sentence, one word, at a time. Our primary connection is not with words but an underlying, almost indefinable emotion that we have always shared. What is not forgotten is the open energy of love that Ulf expresses daily.

2. "I Won't Forget God"

*O*n this particular morning we are both reading from *A Course in Miracles*. Another memorable conversation begins when Ulf looks up from his book and asks me, "Who do you think God is?" This question catches me off guard. Searching for a general answer, I speak of how ancient cultures such as the Egyptians, the Mayans or American Indians gave a revered status to images they saw as powerful, like the sun, or monuments. Others say we cannot see God. Ulf then asks, "Why can't I see God?" I am beginning to get a better understanding of the need for religious cultures to have physical symbols that represent such a vast, abstract idea as God. My personal concept does not translate to form. It's the recognition of a connection from within to an infinite energy. So how do I translate that for Ulf? I then suggest to him, "God's energy is like the light coming through the floor lamp by your chair. We cannot see the electricity coming through the light bulb, but the light shows us the evidence of it. We might say our body is the lamp and when we allow God to shine through us, we turn on the light." Ulf is listening intently as I continue. I then unplug the lamp and say, "If that light represents God, then anger unplugs that energy in us, so the light cannot come through. When we do not unplug the lamp with unloving words or thoughts, the light is there for all to see." Ulf gets the message and says, in a contemplative voice, "When I let God shine through me, then I'm happy." He then asks, "How do we know when we unplug our lamp?" I said, "I'm not sure. We'll just have to wait and find out."

Later that day, Ulf provides his own answer. He becomes agitated because he is unable to find his reading glasses. In the middle of castigating himself, he stops and says in a light-hearted way, "I think I just unplugged my lamp!" I consider that a lesson well learned. If we would all just keep our lamps plugged in, this would be a more peaceful world!

In contrast to being the "light," Ulf and I begin to discuss the ego's energy, which we define, in its simplest form, as the source of his negative feelings. These feelings give Ulf a sense of power. I ask if he recognizes the difference in energy when he feels agitated and angry from when he feels calm and peaceful. (This is not a new topic for us.) I say to him, "Flex your arm muscles and allow the energy to surface." After doing so, Ulf declares in a deep voice and with a stern look, "I feel so powerful!" He likes to play-act. I ask him, "How do you *want* to feel?" "Peaceful," he replies. Peace is a word he often uses and relates to the feeling it brings him. I say, "If you want to feel peaceful and your ego says be angry, who do you think is in charge?" A quizzical look comes over his face as he absorbs this question. Ulf then relaxes his arms, and in a softer voice says, "My ego is playing tricks on me. It made me think I was in charge. Now I have a choice!" We agree that our real power is being able to become aware of the feelings then choose what we want to experience. Each choice has a different outcome. I say to Ulf, "The ego is not a "bogey-man." It is something we made up and can unmake."

After considering our conversation for a while, Ulf says, "The Ego does not want us to think like God. It gets us from inside and wants to be in charge. When I get angry and say stupid things, I forget about God." I say, "The ego is like the fog that hides the mountains from our vision, then drifts away." Ulf replies, "My ego does not want me to see God."

That evening, Ulf and I watch the movie, *A Beautiful Mind*, where Russell Crowe plays John Nash, the brilliant scientist who lost his mind. I put the movie on hold several times as we discuss the strange things the mind does, like Ulf forgetting his past. He says, "It doesn't matter as long as I don't forget God." Ulf's beautiful voice and sincere expression give his simple responses an element of authority.

Reviewing in my mind the conversations we had that day, beginning with Ulf's inquiry about God, I was moved by the simple insights that unfolded from that question. Ulf's ability to deduce this complex concept to its simplest form says to me that he also has a "Beautiful Mind."

3. "God Listens When I Smile"

One day, while we were still living in Sedona, Ulf became grumpy. I said, "Take a walk and talk to God." When he returned he seemed to be in a better mood. I asked if he had talked to God. He said, "Yes." I asked, "What did God say?" Ulf replied, "He said to smile." I asked Ulf what he thought smiling does for him. He said, "If you smile, you will feel better inside." He paused then added, "You can't be angry and smile at the same time." Since then, smiling has been a big part of what he feels we all should do.

Several months later, Ulf and I are on a flight from Arizona to California. After the plane lands and everyone is standing in the aisle waiting for the door to open, Ulf lifts his arm up to get a bag down. He pauses mid-air, looks under his arm at an older, Latino gentleman, sitting all alone about three rows back. Everyone in the aisle follows his gaze. Ulf says to the man, "You would feel much better if you smile." The man looks up, surprised at being noticed, and begins to smile; everyone else begins to smile, then to laugh. The energy in the plane lightens with laughter. Ulf proceeds to get his bag.

Our eventual move to California necessitates going to the DMV to register our car. We are directed to another office. The small, open office has several uniformed Officers and a Secretary on duty. After I complete our business I am in a hurry to leave. Ulf, however, has other plans. He walks to the counter and tells a very stern-looking Officer that he should smile. Ulf proceeds to say, "When I smile, I feel good all over." I watch as the Officer goes from an incredulous look to I'm sure, thinking, "Is this guy dangerous?" His secretary is doubled over in quiet laughter. Finally the Officer begins to smile. Ulf said, "Now don't you feel better?" He's not in the least shy about spreading this message to anyone who will listen.

That afternoon we made one of our frequent trips to Safeway where Ulf enjoys sharing his energy with the customers. Standing in the checkout line behind us is a big bruiser motorcycle guy, tattoos and all. Ulf, being fairly tall himself looks up at him and says, "You'd be much happier if you smiled." I silently cringe. This man looks at Ulf, who appears very presentable, with a baffled look on his face. He then begins to crack a smile, then laughs, along with everyone else in line. Ulf smiles and says, "I told you so!" It's never dull!

Ulf's comments on God can also produce smiles and, sometimes, laughter. We recently attended a lovely wedding lunch in the Napa Valley with my cousins from Texas. Ulf especially remembers Charles, whom we visited on many occasions. Charles sits next to him and they begin talking about God. Charles is a highly regarded doctor who has benefited from, and shared God's bounty. Ulf says to him in a very knowing way, "God has been around a long time and he is a really good person." He paused then added in a serious tone, "He won't call you up and ask you for money!" Charles doubles over in laughter. Everyone at the table laughs.

It never occurred to me to tape Ulf sharing his thoughts from this new perspective that I am writing about (which he is unaware I am doing). Nor did it occur to me that sooner than I could imagine, this would no longer be possible. My friend, Judy Whitson, sent me a digital recorder for just such a purpose. Ulf was unaware that he was being recorded and would not have been interested. After all, recordings are made for *future* listening. Even though I wasn't totally diligent in remembering to use it, I am very grateful to Judy for making it possible to capture Ulf's lovely voice and simple thoughts.

When we arrive home from Safeway, I turn on my little digital recorder and ask Ulf to tell me what he does when we go out and see people, like in the grocery store?

Here is our recorded conversation:

> Ulf: *"I can't tell what I can do because I have to see who I meet. And if there is someone I think might enjoy my giving them a smile and saying some nice things to them, I like to share. Like I said to the man in the wheelchair, "I hope you are having a good day." I give them that feeling and send my energy through to them. I've given something to people, at least in the moment. I'm not trying to say I'm doing it for a lot of the people for a long time."*
>
> (My thought: Could Ulf be sending healing energy to these folks?)
>
> Bev: *"When I see them respond, they look like they got the feeling."*
>
> Ulf: *"I'm not doing much. I like to help them a little bit. It makes me feel peaceful inside."*
>
> Bev: *"This peaceful, healing energy is expressed in many ways through people. Your way of sharing seems to be just right for you."*
>
> Ulf: *"Exactly! I see people who I think might receive me and I smile at them. That's my way of sharing."*
>
> Bev: *"What if you look at somebody and you think they won't accept you?"*
>
> Ulf: *"I'm pretty good about making my choices. I notice if it's someone I think I can deal with or will deal with me.*

If there's someone who is really unhappy, I don't bother them. They've got other things to do to get themselves in order. My job is to try to help if I can."

Ulf sharing his energy in this simple form of expression is just as meaningful to the universe as brilliant words or great accomplishments. We have no concept of how little is asked of us to let the light of God shine through us.

* * * * * * * * *

Today we are talking about a lesson from the *Course*, "There is no peace except the peace of God." Ulf proclaims, "I'm peaceful when I smile because God is listening."

4. Oops, Wrong House

This is the beginning of another day. I am unpacking yet another box from our recent move back to California from Sedona. Ulf is of little help in this move. I ask him to take a box to the kitchen and it ends up in the bedroom. In my rush to try to get everything in its place, I keep repeating, "That's not the kitchen" or "Where is the box you had?" In my own stress, and feeling very alone in this giant task of moving, I forget about Ulf's needs and limitations. When I realize what I am saying and to whom, I attempt to change my mood by laughing in a lighthearted way, "Who cares? Let's have some ice cream." Similar directional things happened much earlier, before his diagnosis, but I just thought he was developing a hearing problem. Little did I know these were symptoms from the small, silent strokes occurring in his brain.

This day is like so many others since we decided to sell our house and move closer to Jenny. I am doing all the work, such as assembling our patio set with ninety small screws, while Ulf is trying to entertain himself. Unbeknownst to me, he decides to take a walk down the street. At this time, Ulf becoming lost was not in our experience, or I would have been better prepared. We are in a large retirement community and the houses look very similar. When Ulf decides to return home, he picks the wrong house.

The doorbell rings and there stands a kindly gentleman neighbor I had not met, with Ulf by his side. They are both smiling and I think 'how nice, Ulf has met someone' and think nothing of it. Later this gentleman tells me Ulf had been to his house, and wondered what he was doing in his house but the neighbor wisely saw his confusion, introduced himself and they began a friendly chat. He asked Ulf if he would like to go walking, to which he readily agreed, thus becoming his buddy. Walking down the street, Ulf recognized our house, so he invited him in to meet me. After the neighbor leaves, I realize I have to keep him close at hand, so I take him into the garage with me to sort out some stuff.

About fifteen minutes later, the inside door to the garage opens and I am staring down the barrel of a drawn pistol. I am dumbstruck. Ulf, however, looks up at the policeman and politely asks, "May I help you?" When the policeman hears that, he suppresses a grin and slowly holsters his gun, all the while talking to the gadget on his right shoulder, assuring dispatch that all is okay. Ulf, being the gentleman he is, walks over to the Officer, smiles, and offers him something to drink. Apparently another neighbor whose house Ulf had tried to enter had called the police. I was grateful to this neighbor because that incident, which embarrassed Ulf, put up an invisible fence that taught him he could not wander off.

It seems there's a new turn in the road everyday and I'm just running to catch up. Hopefully our life will get calmer once we've settled into a routine. This is a "learn as you go" venture into the unknown!

5. Melting the Masks

One of the reasons we have traversed this "mine field" of Ulf's mind and are still standing, is the groundwork laid by *A Course in Miracles*. It has provided us with a common language that he can still grasp and has sustained us throughout his memory loss. In this frame of reference, Ulf understands that the "mind" (memory and cognition) that he has lost is not important because that is not who he is. In fact, he thinks it is actually easier for God to reach him through his "new" mind.

Slowly, with my heart listening to Ulf shedding his old self and opening to his "other mind," I hear the echoes of long forgotten remembrances of my own "other" mind. This other part of his mind validates and rewards him for opening to love and gratitude. I am blessed many times during the day when Ulf expresses gratitude, while others, including professionals, are thinking "how sad, what a tragedy that he is not who he used to be." He often mentions with wonder the beauty of the roses in our garden. He will say, "They keep giving us more roses. Aren't we lucky!" His "This is your best meal!" comments tend to bolster my resolve to make each meal special in some way. In fact, he continually expresses how grateful he is for my being in his life. I only know, at this present moment, that this way of thinking has brought him peace.

Ulf's outward physical presence does not call attention to his limitations, so he is still capable of casual social contact on walks and at the store and likes to engage people in conversation, sharing his thoughts. These brief contacts are important and vital to his ability to share his good feelings with others. He is so intent on doing this that I think he sees it as his mission in life! In his simple way, Ulf is discovering another voice as he awakens to his new world.

We were reading from the *Course* that God's light can shine through you, so, with the recorder running I suggest to Ulf: "When you share your good feelings with people, maybe you're just letting the light shine through."

Ulf nods his head and agrees: "Sure; could be. Anything is possible. A lot of this comes from our wanting to have it and to share it. And when we get into environments, we want to learn what these energies are and get to know what is right for that place. We give from within ourselves."

Later, Ulf is reading another lesson from the *Course* entitled, "God is in the Mind with which I Think." He lowers the book into his lap, looks at me, and asks, "What keeps everyone from thinking like God?" I respond by saying, "I guess that's what we're here to learn." The *Course* invites us to actually unravel our thought system, referred to as the ego, and open ourselves up to seeing the world through peace. It is an ever present guide to us during this time when Ulf's own thought system is "unraveling."

Ulf's identity, created from childhood, is slowly unraveling as the earlier silent strokes begin to affect him. As these stored memories recede, perhaps his "other" mind is beginning to remember another way of being. As I begin, in increments, to shift my perception of who he is, Ulf does not feel alone on his journey. In fact he feels he is becoming *more* than he used to be.

Our use of what we define as the "ego" is helping us overcome the hurdles when frustration and confusion have Ulf in a tight grip of anxiety. During one of these times, I suggest to him, "Exaggerate the feeling of agitation. Now close your eyes and pretend there is a little puppy in a cage inside of you, barking and begging to be released." Ulf put his hands on his chest. Continuing, I say, "Now look inside yourself for the key." Everything is quiet. In a soft voice, I say to him, "When you are ready, slowly unlock the cage and see what happens." After a moment, tears begin to roll down his face and he starts to cry. I softly ask him, "What are you experiencing?" He exclaims, "I feel so free!" As he reaches for my hands I say, "That little animal (energy) has been caged since you were a child and just wanted out. Barking (Ulf's agitation) is his way of getting your attention." From then on, whenever he is agitated, he will later say, "I was just barking ruff, ruff." I reply, "We all do it!

Another time I record this conversation:

Ulf, in a tough sounding voice: *"You'd better be careful of me; I can be really bad. Ruff, ruff!*

Bev: *"You have a really tough ego. Wow!*

Ulf: *"Well, you know, sometimes I feel a little bit upset because something isn't happening the way I want it to. It comes in me and I can feel it and I want to get rid of it.*

Bev: *"We all experience the same thing. It doesn't mean it isn't going to come in. The important thing is to let it go."*

Ulf: *"Well, you don't want to continue doing it. If someone gets a little angry, then they wake up. They stop being angry. When they understand what they've done, they get very upset with themselves. I've done that myself. It's an energy that's gotten into me and wants to push everyone away."*

Bev: *"So maybe the whole objective of the ego is to push people away and be separate!"*

Ulf: *"Absolutely. It's just making noise. It's all negative stuff. And that's why, if peace is part of your thoughts, you let go of that from within you.*

Bev: *"Yes. And the ego doesn't like peace."*

Ulf: *"Because there would be no reason for it to be there. It wouldn't have anything to do. So if I'm not going to be listening to it, the ego is not going to show up inside me. When I am being loving, there's nothing more for it to do. I think the ego is afraid of love."*

* * * * * * * * *

Ulf's ego also goes through periods of fearing "abandonment." During one of these moments of frustration, he looks at me with pleading, sad eyes and says, "You don't love me." I step forward and give him a loving hug, but this is not to be a quick pill of appeasement. He was dropping one of the masks that he felt defined him, one that hides the fear. His willingness to voice this pain is a step toward dissolving it. Most of the story linked to the pain is lost to memory. However, the emotional memory remains.

These masks, which we refer to as the ego, trick us by covering up the pain of the false belief that we are alone in the universe. Our life situations can be ruled by these hidden fears. Ulf is living the awareness that they separate him from his deeper connection to the universe within, such as when he "unplugged" his light. Peeking behind these self-designed masks and experiencing the pain or fear, without the story, can unveil what the mask has prevented us from seeing, our true Self. Ulf did not choose an easy path to that higher connection. Neither did Dr. Jill Bolte Taylor who, in her book *Stroke of Insight,* writes so dramatically about the insights that occurred to her during and after her stroke. She said that when her cognition began to return, so did some of the emotional programs. Her way of dealing with these emotions, which were in stark contrast to her newly discovered "right" brain, was to wait silently for ninety seconds for this response to dissolve.

It is amazing to witness the results of peeling away the layers of our false selves that we have come to cherish. Recently Ulf said, "I don't need the ego's energy," and added with a "ruff, ruff" and a smile, "my mind is simple and straight-forward."

6. Exploring the Unknown

*M*any years ago, I was working in a treatment center with children who were loosely labeled "psychotic." I observed moments of fear and trepidation in the children. They believed they had done something wrong and that being sent away from their families defined them. That definition made it difficult for them to trust any evidence that proved otherwise. Life had been pretty tough on these kids, so they were hesitant to try anything new. Where there is fear, there is no laughter.

They do not teach "having fun and laughing" at the universities, so I had to invent ways of changing the children's experience. I used simple approaches like putting about eight of them in a van and driving around, looking to discover something new. The Center was in a lovely rural, mountainous environment, so when we reached a crossroad, we would vote on which way to go. After making the chosen turn, we would look for the surprises we never would have seen if we had not turned. "Oh, look at that little calf with his mother drinking from the stream" or "See that tree with three trunks?" There were lively discussions about what we saw and how much fun it was to explore. Everyone was challenged to point out something new. In their excitement, they forgot, for a time, their labeled limitations.

Ulf experiences similar challenges as his world begins to get smaller. No one calls him anymore. He goes to the mailbox several times a day to see if there is something with his name on it. These simple things that often go unnoticed are reminders to him of his limited contact with others. To expand his experience, we get in the car and see what adventure awaits us. Ulf always lightens up in anticipation of whatever we may find. While driving, he enthusiastically points out a large flying bird hovering over the vineyards, or horses feeding on the long grass. Yesterday, we went looking for one thing and instead found a Honey Bee House where we learned about the life of bees, then bought some honey. After watching the scurrying of the bees in their hives, Ulf said, "They are very busy bees! Aren't we having fun?" I laughed, "We sure are!" Exploring is a fun adventure." Every time we leave the house, we wonder what's going to happen next. As Ulf becomes open to exploring the unknown, his small world expands.

Ulf loves to observe nature from our patio. Whenever the cloud formations change, or a flock of birds fly by, or a deer turns and looks at him, he marvels at the surprises nature brings us. Something that was unknown a moment ago is suddenly there before us.

Our dear friend Haizen, an amateur astronomer who lives in Sedona, introduced Ulf to the wonders of the sky. Haizen is a gentle soul who observed the enthusiasm in Ulf and invited him to join in the vast exploration of nightly beauty. Remembering this exploration with his friend, Ulf checks the night sky to see what is happening with the moon and stars. His world is getting larger.

Jenny brought over some small, brightly colored and oddly shaped blocks. It takes Ulf just a few minutes to get over his "this is for children" judgment and he begins to build two cities, one on each placemat. He then wonders who will come and live in them. I said, "Anyone you want. You can imagine anything." "But it's not real," he said with a little smile. I said, "Look at the painting of Venice over our fireplace. That is actually the artist's imagination. Your imagination can create whatever you want." He then asks, "What if they don't get along?" I said, "You may have to become their teacher." Later, when he said they were indeed not getting along, I suggested that he go talk to them. I walked away, but within earshot, I could hear him talking to "them" about love. He then put his hands on each "city" mat and closed his eyes. I think he was sharing his "light" energy with "them."

Ulf's Cities

7. GHOSTS OF THE PAST

My book, *Grains of Sand*, tells, in poetic phrasing, of the journey of Innocence, born into this reality looking for Love, forgetting that we *are* Love. Pain and disillusionment follow as we awaken to a world of separation. We weave many masks into the fabric of this uncertain and often frightening beginning. These vaguely hidden masks then become our identity, which I often refer to as the ego.

Some of our masks receive applause, while others draw negativity upon us. The children I worked with attracted the latter. Having learned Gestalt techniques from Dr. Fritz Perls, who founded Gestalt Therapy, I used this as a form of play with children. One incident that comes to mind was with a boy named Michael, an eight-year-old school terror whose father was an alcoholic. He told me one day, "There's a monster in the hallway." I suggested he invite him into the room. He said, "Oh no, there's too much light!" A couple of days later I said, "Would you like to play a pretend game? Just pretend to put the monster in that chair in front of you." Michael screwed up his face in a grimace. I assured him, "We won't really bring him in. This is just a game of pretend." He agreed. I saw him look at the little chair and then all the way up to the ceiling. I said, "Wow! That's a big monster. What would you like to say to him?" This little boy, this "school terror," said in a tiny, squeaky voice, "My name is Michael. You are very big. Please don't hurt me." After a few minutes, I suggested he sit in the monster's chair and pretend to be the monster. With lots of hesitation, he eased into the chair and began to morph into this big energy with a tough voice, saying to Michael's empty chair, "You're stupid. No one likes you. You can't even read." He kicked the chair over. I said to the 'monster,' "You want to be kinder to Michael. He's a nice guy!" We did not dwell on the episode but some time later, Michael said, "Do you remember the monster? Well he's my friend now and lets me hug him." Very soon after resolving this conflict within himself, his teacher saw a calmer child. The central theme of the *Course* is Forgiveness. It is the recognition that what we judge outside ourselves is just a mirror of our inward struggle. Michael, in his poignantly innocent and graphic way, dissolved that polarity within himself.

I've witnessed the polarities within Ulf between his open loving self and his agitated, constricted self as his cognitive abilities decrease. The fact that he is aware of these two aspects may be defining his spiritual path. These symbols of separation begin to rise like ghosts in the mist, chanting all the fables of his past, "Who am I, why am I here, what is happening to me? I'm so alone." He is traversing his "Valley of the Shadow of Death." Death symbolizes the loss of *who he thinks he is.* Ulf's mantra through all this is "I want Peace." That persistent call for peace tells me that somewhere within himself, Ulf is seeking to dissolve those seeming opposites into Oneness.

This is Ben's story. He was sent to me at age 13 as a result of his response to his parent's divorce. He was not acting out but was somewhat disoriented. Art is a good medium for children to peek inside. The insights that come from this experience are greater than anything I could imagine, so I kept a large roll of butcher paper and drawing pens handy. Drawing was something Ben relished. One day on a large piece of paper, he began drawing two sizable trashcans with a hand coming out of each. One of the hands was very distorted. I rarely said anything about a drawing that was too definitive, so I said, "Ben, those hands look different from each other." He said, "You would be different too if you had been buried for three years." I said, "How wonderful that he is coming out of the garbage can. What do you think he would like to see?" On another large paper he drew this beautiful, peaceful garden with a pond. After that, there were no more drawings of garbage cans, tombstones and scary family portraits. Interestingly enough, one of Fritz Perl's books is titled, In and Out of the Garbage Can.

My long interest in the creative imaginings of our minds that invites us to play is what I bring to our present experience.

As Ulf has become more challenged, these experiences with children allowed me to provide the creative stage for Ulf to express himself. His awakening that silent, enthusiastic voice within is a bright light in those times when I feel 'burned out'. The result has been many precious moments. Maybe we should all look for that kid within!

8. DISCOVERING SELF

"*O*nly Presence can free you of the ego, and you can only be present now, not yesterday or tomorrow. Only Presence can undo the past in you and thus transform your state of consciousness." Ulf has been reading aloud from Eckhart Tolle's book, *A New Earth*. When I ask him what thoughts he has about the book, he says, "It brings all the elements together. We begin to learn as we start going in. We need to be aware that there are things that go on within us. We will all experience a lot of different things at different times in our lives and one day we will learn it is not important." Ulf gives an interesting twist to the meaning of the words and truly enjoys expressing them. It is an extension of his desire to share the energy he feels coming through him.

Several methods have helped us along the way to understand the emotional polarities Ulf is experiencing and to discover our loving Self. Soon after his diagnosis of dementia/sleep apnea six years ago, we had the good fortune to attend seminars teaching The Sedona Method, a simple way of releasing emotions in which stories were not allowed. This is not a "who did what to whom" exercise in futility. It aided both of us in realizing that releasing these cumbersome emotions can be simple and swift when disconnected from the stories that flow through our emotional mind. When Ulf felt agitated, he would put on his headset and listen to one of the cd's on releasing anger. It was extremely helpful to him because it did not require resurrecting memories to be effective.

The men of Ulf's generation are not usually open to dealing with emotions. Ulf's willingness to explore this aspect of himself is very endearing to me. This ability has been essential in managing our current situation. He would cry out, "I feel so alone. I have no value," as the realization that he is not the person he used to be begins to dawn on him. The *Course* says, "You who hold your brother's hand also hold mine, for when you join each other you were not alone." I sense that truth daily. When Ulf and I join with each other, we both experience another, underlying energy. Ulf often takes my hand as we sit on the sofa and says, "Feel that energy flowing through us!" We seem to be sharing something together that we did not experience by ourselves, so he no longer feels alone.

As Ulf and I can attest, when we begin the unmasking process of discovering our Self, the emotional programs we have wrapped around our life stories begin to emerge. Ulf's feelings of abandonment and my sense of loss of the person I had known are testimonies to that truth. For some, this is a voluntary mission, but for others it can be involuntary and frightening. We have built a fortress shielding our Spirit—which needs no protection—from these emotions woven into memories. A thousand stories of our life, stone upon stone, can be built upon a single emotion like anger, fear, grief, or guilt. One day this fortress will come tumbling down. Maybe dementia, or "forgetting," is the "Locomotive Express" to our Universal Mind. We could consider it as one path to spiritual freedom.

This note, written two years ago in Sedona, speaks to Ulf's early desire to come to terms with his new identity:

Dearest Bev,

I have been reading Tolle's book entitled "Stillness Speaks."

I found the chapter entitled "Who you truly are." It

addresses a subject that will help me, and maybe you, to clear up the continuing question, "Who am I and Why?" If you want to we can discuss when I return.

By the way I am fully restored through my conversation with our close friend "GOD."

Love you, Ulf

BE BACK FROM MY WALK ABOUT 9 O'CLOCK

9. Row, Row Your Boat

"Row, row, row your boat, gently down the stream.
Merrily, merrily, merrily, merrily, Life is but a Dream."

*E*very day is a new adventure for Ulf and me. Even if we are just going to the store, there is something new to observe or someone to make smile. Today we venture to Spring Lake, a ten-minute drive from our house, and rent a rowboat. Ulf was on a rowing team at school and often went rowing with the children. Curious to observe if he still has any memory of how to proceed, I do not have to wait long. Ulf immediately begins to give me specific instructions. He lets me know in no uncertain terms that he is in charge, even as the boat circles for the third time after we leave the shore. Ulf is flustered but determined to take control of the situation, talking the whole time about how this should be done. There is a commanding tone in his voice.

As the boat finds its direction, his sense of accomplishment radiates from his face and we set off on our journey across the lake.

Gently rowing along the shores, we see ducks scurrying about as we drift slowly under the tree branches providing shade. We see clusters of flying insects and bugs floating on the water's surface. As Ulf attempts to navigate close to a shore hideaway, he allows me to assist him. It is interesting for me to witness the process as he tries to assimilate old memories into a present action that has to be executed immediately. I watch as his arms and hands on the oars go into automatic response to a remembered skill. A part of Ulf that had been dormant is coming alive and he feels the exhilaration.

After a while, he becomes accustomed to the feeling of being in charge and is delighted with this new authority over a small aspect of his life.

Every day is a new adventure for Ulf

As we quietly drift under the shade of the trees surrounding the lake, tears come to my eyes as I realize how seldom Ulf must experience this feeling of being in control of his life. So much decision-making has been turned over to me. It gives me a graphic understanding of the frustration Ulf must feel when he is unable to respond to simple instructions, or a desire to perform the chores that would allow him to participate more fully in our daily life.

We have finally come to the "Gently down the stream" part of this life experience. The kid part of me really resonates to the "merrily, merrily" verse as we play on the putting green or build block cities or go looking for adventure. My natural playfulness brings me closer to where Ulf is residing as we joke and tease one another. I am grateful for the opportunity to live with an open heart as I share his boat with him. He is truly my teacher on this journey toward Innocence.

When I hear the dire tones of a doctor's prediction of what our future holds, or when well-meaning friends say, "This is only going to become more difficult," staying in the present moment becomes even more vital to our experience. If I pollute the "Present Moment" with fear, then I lose it. Maybe my silliness reflects my understanding of the *Course* expressed in the last line of the verse of the song, "Life is but a Dream." If that is indeed true, we should all lighten up and row more gently and merrily through life.

10. Fun at the Pharmacy

*O*ur move from familiar surroundings has been difficult for Ulf to assimilate. It has been necessary for him to join me for my doctor visits or a wait in the pharmacy. For that matter, it also includes shopping for clothes on the run—no dressing room, hairdresser or dentist. No movies.

Moving from Sedona, we left friends behind, so there is no one we know who can stay with Ulf even for short periods of time. Eventually, I did meet a lovely woman, Lily, who lives in our community and takes Ulf for walks. He is delighted with her and it gives me an hour of "down time." She is very patient as he speaks to and pets every animal they pass and she redirects him if he checks someone else's mailbox, thinking it is ours. Being aware of his level of functioning, I have become skilled at distracting him away from "trouble." It is a "learn as you go" process. However, it is always foremost in my mind to treat his behavior as normal (which for him it is). In fact he behaves quite normally for his condition.

One day while waiting for a prescription to be filled at the pharmacy, we are standing in line. Ulf looks back at all the people seated and announces in his forthright, lovely deep voice, "I hope everyone here is having a wonderful day." This bored group suddenly lights up and put their magazines down as he gets their attention. He continues, "It's up to you to have the day you want. I'm having a good day." I think, "Good grief, he is sounding like a motivational speaker." Naturally, the people begin to smile and chat with each other about this amusing guy. It really loosens up the group. One woman loudly states, "I want what he's taking!" Everyone laughs and agrees.

A man asks Ulf, "Is your wife having a good day?" He responds, "When I have a good day, she has a good day." That brings another chuckle. The man gives his wife a knowing smile and the remarks continue. By the time we leave, Ulf has a roomful of new friends. This event is amusing to me because Ulf is not trying to be funny. To him, he is just making straightforward statements of fact.

What makes the experience even more interesting to me is that in Ulf's "past life" he never would have dreamt of saying such things spontaneously to a group of people he did not know. Those who have known Ulf see him as being very much an unpretentious, reserved gentleman, a trait he never lost. He is a friendly, but private person and not especially humorous. A book that brings laughter to him is *Scandinavian Humor and Other Myths,* with pictures of two "take no prisoners" women on the front cover.

It is increasingly natural for me now to just go along with whatever Ulf does—actions that would appear abnormal to most folks—and take it all in stride. The fact that his behavior is within very acceptable bounds makes it easier. I view it as another aspect of Ulf expressing what he did not previously allow himself to experience. It is a fresh and new canvas for him to paint on, which he does enthusiastically. My acceptance of his behavior is validating for him, so he does not feel left out and separate. He is also very sensitive to other people's feelings, so he is conscious of the appropriateness of his behavior in terms of comfort to others.

However, Ulf does paint some challenging scenes for me on the flipside of that canvas. The flipside occurs while shopping for shoes. Fortunately, we are in a self-service store with high partitions displaying rows of shoes. We find a pair suitable for him. There is only one problem. He loudly declares, "I'm not taking off my shoes." With a little coaxing, he finally takes off one shoe, but not the other, and begrudgingly tries on one of the new shoes. He then announces in a stern voice that he is not taking off the new shoe. I can feel my teeth clenching and the blood rising to my head, which signals the end of my patience. In an equally stern voice, I say, "Ok, let's go!" I pick up the remaining shoes and head for the cash register where a startled young woman just takes the money and, to her credit, says nothing.

* * * * * * * * * *

This is yet another form of Ulf's expressive outlet. Every painting is different. Every experience has its particular texture; some disturbing, some humorous, but always authentic to the person he has become.

11. Back to the Red Rocks

*U*lf and I recently drove to the Sedona Red Rock Country for our first visit since moving to California six months ago. We visited the condo we had bought for vacation rental on a small nine-hole golf course with an extraordinary view. The fifteen years we spent living there are full of memories of friends, events, dinner parties and, of course, hiking the trails. It is a challenge to take Ulf from a familiar routine and surroundings to a place that has become sketchy in his memory. However, I am surprised how his memory begins filling in the blanks as he meets old friends and sees again the incredible views. Ulf remembers his good friends even while forgetting events and places, which have become irrelevant to him.

There is one event Ulf does remember. While driving through the red rocks, he tells me he remembers seeing them from the sky. I asked him about it. He said, "We flew over this in an airplane." This turns out to be true. Ron and Nancy, with whom we shared many child-rearing episodes, came to visit us. Ulf remembers that when Ron retired from the research lab he and Nancy bought a Cessna and flew it to Sedona and Ron gave him a thrilling birds-eye view flying over the red rocks.

Ulf and I stayed with our friend Pene Walsh, who for many years shared our home on her yearly trips from Australia. Whenever she visited us, we spent hours enjoying the view from our deck while sipping coffee or wine and discussing topics like the "meaning of life," being open to new experiences and lessons yet to be learned. Great fun! She eventually moved to Sedona. During our visit, Pene took Ulf walking on his favorite red rock trail, which recalled for him enjoyable memories of being in nature.

One of the friends that Ulf remembered with fondness was Max, the then Unity Church minister in Sedona. We had met Max Lafser and his wife Rama Vernon the first week we moved to Sedona and remained close friends. Ulf reads the Unity Daily Word magazine, which is often nestled in his back pocket, a ready reminder of how he wants his day to be. Max shared this with me recently: "I never felt I had to preach, teach or do anything more than be with Ulf. Actually I always felt he was the one to teach me... not with words, but with his inclusive, quiet nature. It is a blessing for a minister to find places, people one doesn't have to do something for, or be anything more than the quiet self. That is the gift Ulf brought to me."

Occasionally, Ulf's feeling of being disoriented returns. Like the captain of his rowboat, he tries to take charge of what is happening around him after arriving in a foreign land. He responds to these reactions by saying, "It's the ego trying to take charge of me." I tell him, "We all get a little anxious when we are in unfamiliar territory."

We make an appointment to see Dr. Sung Lee who created the Brain Well Center, www.brainwellcenter.com. Ulf enrolled in his program before we moved from Sedona. He felt compatible with Dr. Lee's calm and accepting presence, which he remembers. Initially Dr. Lee did a Brain Map on Ulf; a simplified EEG that tells us what parts of the brain may be over or under active or out of balance. Based on the Brain Map, Dr. Lee then developed a training plan to provide advanced brainwave biofeedback to Ulf. Sensors, placed on the scalp, read electrical energy from the brain and send it to a computer program, which transforms it into soft, musical tones. The tones are transmitted back to the patient (usually with eyes closed) through headphones,

As an observer, it is fascinating to see the visual transformation of the calming of energy on the computer screen. It is reflected in Ulf as I see his face and body relax. During his initial ten sessions before we left Sedona, I noticed a lessening of the repetitive abandonment theme of, "you are going to leave me," which had escalated during the awesome process of packing up to move. I note a general calming of Ulf's overall demeanor. In the two hours we are with Dr. Lee on our return visit, he does many protocols and Ulf responds well to the retraining. When the brain is calm, cognition and awareness are heightened. Maybe Brain Mapping is actually hi-tech meditation! Ulf relates well to Dr. Lee's gentle manner.

While Dr. Lee was working with Ulf, he put me into another room and wired me for a different experience. The impulses put me into an altered meditative state as he led me through a guided imagery. He said, "You are emerging from a wooded area into a clearing with a cottage. Go up the stairs and open the door. There are three doors. Behind the first one are your fears." I open it and see little gremlins scurrying around. Dr. Lee said, "Gather them up and put them down the chute." Not very scary. Behind the second door is Gratitude. I slowly open the door, expecting to see the many people for whom I'm grateful. I am totally unprepared for the angelic looking person on a stairway whom I know as Margit! Tears begin to flow. The awareness that we are all on a mutually supportive path to love shifts my perception of this person with whom it had been difficult for me to have a relationship. In that instant I realized that Margit was my partner in our family drama! After all, we are all joined in spirit. I guess forgiveness is the realization that the roles we play are just illusions created to free each other, if we choose. The third door is the future. I see Ulf and me holding hands as we emerge from the forest into a brilliant sunset. This experience, guided by Dr. Lee, opened me to another dimension of reality that was very "real." It is beyond the thinking mind.

Ulf visits with another friend and buddy, Haizen, the amateur astronomer who introduced him to the wonders of the night sky. He is also an astrologer. We had the pleasure of meeting his lovely girlfriend who brought a sparkle to his eyes. While still living in Sedona, along with pointing out the planets, Haizen would often take Ulf to the local cafe where there was live music, and once, even belly dancing! With incredible sensitivity, he gave Ulf a much needed guy's night out. Ulf felt appreciated and "normal" because Haizen genuinely enjoyed his company. What a beautiful expression of friendship! Music was central to Haizen's early life when he played saxophone with Stan Kenton. Listening to him play at a memorial for a friend touched everyone deeply. It was like listening to the sounds of velvet. Ulf once said to Haizen, in a very casual and matter-of-fact way, "I went to that big guy in the sky (the moon) with a small group who asked me to join them to help lift and move things. There are a lot of things in the sky that we are unable to see from here. The moon is just one big rock and not interesting but looking back to where we live, (Earth), was very beautiful. We were all joined together." Some of the astronauts said exactly the same thing on returning from their trip to the moon!

All things considered, our trip to Sedona was a good opportunity for Ulf to be reminded of a few of his long time friendships. Of course, the lovely red rock vistas are literally unforgettable. One of the memories that linger for me are the thoughtful notes Ulf would leave for me before going on a walk. This is one of those notes he wrote:

Just a moment of thought for you, my Dearest Bev!

As I walked this morning I had my conversation with God.

As I walked home You came with me and I thought of all the wonderful actions, thoughtfulness, kindness that I and so many others receive from you daily.

YOU ARE THE BEST WIFE ANY MAN EVER HAD!!!

LOVE,

YOU KNOW WHO!!!!

THE COUNT

12. Who am I?

*P*reparing dinner is foremost in my mind when Ulf begins his "you don't love me" mantra. "That is not who you are," I say rather sternly to him. "Then who am I?" he demands in a loud voice. This repetitive mind recording has been playing in the late afternoon for the past few days. It continues for about thirty-minutes, then he calms down and talks about what he just experienced. With his face tightly clenched, he says, "The ego just grabbed me and I felt everything tighten inside of me. I don't want to be that person. I want to be kind and loving. How can I stop it?"

He had read, in Eckhart Tolle's book, *Stillness Speaks*, that the ego's response is activated by a thought from the past and is usually an exaggeration of the current situation. Tolle said the first step in removing that thought is to become aware that this energy does exist. The second step is to have this awareness occur while still in the clutches of the experience. When we do that, we become the observer and the attachment is weakened. Apparently Ulf got the message because he is able to do just that in the middle of his emotional "recording." He suddenly stops the rhetoric and, with a startled look, as if awakening from a dream, declares, "Something just happened! I see what I'm doing. I heard myself talking nonsense again." I said, "You did it! You heard your Spirit through the noise of your ego! What an incredible thing you just did!" And indeed it was. Ulf said with a big smile, "I'm free." Ulf had brought his awareness of his ego to the present moment.

The primary function of our thought system, which created the ego, is to amplify the separation with other bodies, a group or an ideology. There always has to be an "other." It can be expressed as pride, accomplishment, anger, fear or hate. The purpose is to use these self-taught mechanisms to push away and distance our selves from each other. This only has power over us because we have become identified and attached to it. It is who we think we are. However, we are *not* who we think we are. When that energy is freed from the confines of our thinking mind with its repetitive stories, it removes the blocks to our experience of Love.

Ulf and I have been witness to this separation theme playing out in many forms since his diagnosis. A friend of ours once confessed that she had an aversion to anyone with a disability, both physical and mental, like Ulf's. I was initially taken aback, but quickly reminded myself of the people in whom I sensed a silent aversion that was subtle, but nonetheless there. As Ulf's ability to engage in an on-going conversation with anyone besides me begins to decline, I notice how people in the medical profession, especially men, remain distant from Ulf, as if he's not in the room. With Ulf present, one doctor said, "I wish I had known Ulf "before." He could not see past his diagnosis, the reflection of spirit in Ulf *now*. There were exceptions to this. When we were still in Sedona, Dr. Don Curran, Ulf's sleep specialist, who is also a psychiatrist, was especially sensitive and personally acknowledged Ulf for who he presently was. He would speak directly to him and joust man-to-man, saying, "Us guys have to stick together," so by the time the appointment was concluded, Ulf was bolstered in a way I could never have done for him. Dr. Diana Hydzik was also our doctor and good friend. She followed our medical journey from a holistic perspective and treated Ulf with the utmost respect. In discussing medical options, she would include Ulf in the conversation in a way he could comprehend.

So here I am, witnessing the unraveling of this intricate system of thought and emotion. I see it as Ulf's heroic journey rather than a disability. The most courageous journey anyone can make is to go through the initial pain and suffering we inflict on ourselves as we detach from our personal stories. This usually occurs with dramatic changes in our life. When we detach, there is no longer any pain.

I'm reminded of the Tibetan Monks who spend long periods of time painstakingly creating highly intricate sand Mandalas, then ceremoniously sweeping the sand when they are finished. That is a symbolic lesson in non-attachment and impermanence. Resistance to "sweeping away" the false self we have spent a lifetime creating, delays our inevitable choice to transform this expression of limitation into a fuller experience of our true Self. Making this choice is the reason we are here and the single, most powerful and only decision we ever really make.

13. I Don't Understand

For the umpteenth time, I am explaining to Ulf that there are three garbage trucks, one for each of the garbage cans, and not to bring the cans back to the house until they are emptied. He smiles and says, "I don't understand what you are saying, but if it makes you happy, just keep on talking." Well, I stop talking and start laughing.

In my new world with Ulf, language has taken on a different meaning. Simplicity is the key. Talking or writing about philosophical or spiritual subjects is like painting a verbal picture or a word mosaic. Words are a creative tool for me, and when I am writing I feel connected with that energy. Living with a man who had a stroke in the part of his brain that affects receptive auditory ability, has forced me to rethink the art of communication.

Ulf and I do have conversations on subjects like energy... God... Spirit... in which Ulf seems to have a simple understanding that is much better than taking directions about garbage cans. I guess subjects like Spirit and things we cannot see are filed in our "right brain." For instance, Ulf asks again about talking to God. He refers to God as someone outside himself, to which I reply, "Imagine that God speaks to the Spirit *inside* you and is a part of you, even your brain!" He laughs and says, "I'm glad there's something up there." That thought intrigues him and I observe him talking to himself and pointing to his head. It seems that God just got a lot more personal. Ulf's understanding of that kind of direct connection with something "invisible" continues to surprise me. He seems to grasp something we all struggle with and try to use words to explain.

This morning Ulf was reading aloud from the *Course*. When he finished, I asked him to tell me what he had just read. He said, "Most of what we think we know isn't true." He had captured, very simply, the meaning of words he had just read.

Communication is an essential part of the structure of our identity. We express, either in words or thoughts, the stories driving our experiences. This constant buzz in our heads usually encompasses a belief in attack and defense, right and wrong, good and bad. If our words do not express the Love within us, which does not judge or polarize, they have no real meaning. I think that is what Ulf is demonstrating. As his busy thoughts have quieted and his comprehension of words has simplified, Ulf is experiencing more of a loving presence within himself. How strange that we make the judgment that he is the one "losing" his mind. I am increasingly aware of the peace that comes from quieting the mind and talking in simple terms. When Ulf says, "I don't understand," perhaps he is speaking a much greater truth than talking about garbage cans.

14. OUT TO SEA

*O*ur dining table faces a large window framing a lovely view of the mountains beyond the rose garden. This day, Ulf is casually eating while watching the high clouds drift by. The scene mirrors a feeling of contentment as we eat our lunch. Looking out the window between bites, Ulf dreamily says, "I think I'm going to kill myself." Equally as casual, I simply mutter "Um," and continue eating.

Ulf is becoming increasingly aware of his shrinking world. Although he is physically fit, he cannot walk down the street alone and hope to return to our house. So he sometimes wonders aloud, "Why am I still here?" To me this is a very valid question, one that any of us would ask if on a similar downhill path.

When Ulf makes this statement over lunch, I swallow and say, "How do you plan to do it?" He replies, "I'm going to swim out to sea and not come back." To which I respond, "That'll sure do it for you!" I take another bite of chicken salad and then comment that there is only one problem with his plan, the ocean is over an hour away and he does not drive. Ulf gets this thoughtful look on his face as he stares out at the mountains. He then lights up as a solution appears to him. He reaches in his back pocket, takes out his billfold where he keeps his Neptune Society (Crematorium) card and says "These guys will take me out to sea!" I burst into laughter and say, "Ulf, you have to be dead *first!*" He had remembered the conversation when we bought the plan that we could have a burial at sea. I would have loved hearing that phone conversation with the Neptune Society!

As in all conversations we have about death, dying, the hereafter, and why any of us is here anyway, this one is treated as a very natural curiosity we all have but rarely discuss. These discussions are not morbid and do not have any undertones of foreboding.

In contrast to "ending it," Ulf more often sees life in terms of energy that he calls God's energy. It is the name he gives to something that he experiences as a part of himself. Because he *feels* the energy, it is very real to him and his instinct is to share it with the people he meets walking in the park. After lunch, we decide that while we are still alive, we might as well enjoy it, so we go to the park. It is Ulf's favorite place to share his energy with dogs and the people walking them, touching each with his love. This sharing of his love brightens his smile and puts a spring in his step. Any more thoughts of death will just have to wait!

15. Christmas Time

*C*hristmas is in three days. Colored lights and Santa with his reindeer line the quiet streets in our community and the stores are bustling with last minute shoppers. These symbols of joy are reminders of the sadness that occasionally creeps up on me. Perhaps the invitation to be joyful is acting as a catalyst to bring up my memories of a very difficult time that I would rather forget. I know (but am obviously not practicing) that there is no such thing as "forgetting," just repressing, avoiding, or pushing away. So maybe *my* Christmas message is to look straight into the past from the present. Writing is my therapeutic and creative messenger to myself, as this journey is revealed to me step by step. For this healing process, I will share some of those feelings that want to be freed and see where it leads me.

My action plan for dealing with Ulf's situation began in 2004. At this time all my instincts were on high alert. This left little time for me to assess my emotional reactions to the time bomb that had been activated by the "dementia" diagnosis. There were times I would stop in the middle of a grocery aisle and begin to cry. The grief of seeing the person you dearly love slowly disappear is heart wrenching.

There were a multitude of emotions and adjustments during this time of uncertainty. Ulf was frantically grappling with the disorienting changes in his world and I was simply trying to make sense of it all. This was one of those "trying to stay afloat on the lake when the dam breaks" periods. It is better known as a crisis!

There was little or no support for me because people tend to retreat from an impending flood. Even my best friend, Ulf, was not available to help. I felt alone and thus went into survival mode. None of the lessons dear to my heart about a Higher Source, God or Miracles came running to my rescue. My heart was heavy and I felt separate and abandoned by the very sources that spoke of unity. Everything that had inspired me only served to remind me of what was missing. I was not interested in the "big" picture but just in my little world that was falling apart. I was walking through my "valley of the shadow of death," as it were. Even my own much earlier impending death to cancer did not have this sort of impact on me. Nothing in my experience equaled this inability to control my circumstances, even though I knew intellectually, that control was an illusion.

Much of my life has been filled with stimulating, externally directed events. This sense of being alone, however, has also been an opportunity for me to look within to unravel the unnecessary clutter of my own mind. I am experiencing both the restrictive and disconnect feelings of isolation and the connective, expansive space of peaceful solitude. I have noticed that within that expanded space, I have attracted whatever I need in the moment and the feeling of separation disappears. Ulf is highly sensitive to any shift in energy, so he has been my ever-present teacher in staying "awake."

Revisiting and bringing fresh air to those initial memories has lifted for now, my holiday remorse. I am asking for further guidance in allowing those feelings to be liberated. Awakening to the improbable result of surrendering to "what is," is my Miracle. The transformation from the sense of separation to one of joining is what the Christmas message is about.

A Course in Miracles says, "Watch with me, angels, watch with me today. Let all God's holy Thoughts surround me, and be still with me while Heaven's Son is born. Let earthly sounds be quiet, and the sights to which I am accustomed disappear. Let Christ be welcomed where He is at home. And let Him hear the sounds He understands, and see but sights that show His Father's Love. Let Him no longer be a stranger here, for He is born again in me today."

Christmas Time celebrates the end of separation. We are no longer alone in whatever journey we imagine we take. As this awareness dawns on us, Miracles light our path leading to Peace and Love.

Merry Christmas!

16. It's About Time!

It is New Year's Eve. There is a fire burning in the fireplace, lighted candles are on the dining room table casting a soft glow over our festive meal and crystal champagne glasses are ready for "toasting." Images of Times Square are on television. Ulf asks, "What is the fuss on TV about?" I reply, "It's Times Square celebrating a new year." He looks at me with a puzzled look and asks, "What does that mean?" I quickly realize that this person, who is living in a timeless zone, may be in need of some education about this event celebrating time. I bring the calendar to the table and set out to explain how time progresses from one year to the next. Ulf isn't impressed and asks me to sit down. He then takes my hand, looks deep into my eyes and says in a calm, forthright manner, "Beverly, my sitting here with you, holding your hand, is the only time there is." I look at Ulf in wonder as the profound message of his words touches my heart.

Ulf is now defining this experience from his new frame of reference. For all practical purposes, time has become irrelevant for him but it seems, from his beautiful statement to me, that he is opening the door to a new world.

This New Year's revelation of "time" reminds me of when I was driving along a two-lane road through farm country in the Sonoma Valley where we live. Ulf was looking out the window, watching the cows, horses, fields and vineyards flash by like a five-second slide show. He broke the silence and said, "Time just keeps on changing all the time." For someone who cannot tell time but still wears his watch, even though it has stopped, and cannot remember the "slide show," Ulf's world must be like living inside a kaleidoscope. And yet, he is seeing time for what it really is—illusive, changing and selectively remembered in bits and pieces. Can you believe we insist on constructing and molding our lives around something so impermanent?

When I think of the billions of pixels we have organized into snapshot images since birth and then attached emotions and experiences to these briefly held symbols of our identity, I'm amazed that anyone takes memory seriously. We then create a time line to give us a context in which to file this confetti in one of our brain folders labeled "Memories of the Past."

A Course in Miracles states the illusion of time in many ways: "Time is inconceivable without change, yet holiness does not change.... Change is an illusion." "For what is time without a past and future? It has taken time to misguide you so completely, but it takes no time at all to be what you are.... Take this very instant, now, and think of it as all there is of time." "To learn to separate out this single second, and to experience it as timeless, is to experience yourself as not separate." "The present is the only time there is."

So it seems that the ego's use of time is to remember the *past* in order to create the *future*, which in turn creates the illusion of *change*, which takes *"time."*

The next day, the first of the New Year, we continue our discussion about how to hear God because Ulf is concerned he could not hear Him talking. I say, "Close your eyes and think of peace." After a moment he says, with an element of surprise in his voice, "I can feel it. I feel it *here*," putting his hand on his chest. I say, "That's how God talks to you." He immediately expresses gratitude to me by taking my hand and squeezing it, and says, "It is that simple. Whenever we listen in God's time, which is right now, that brings us peace." To me, Ulf's curiosity in exploring how he can have a direct experience with this larger energy that circumvents time is reflected in his unusual insight when he spoke to me on New Year's Eve. These are not new concepts for Ulf, just a new level of awareness. His changing concepts of time, however, can be confusing when the rest of us are living in a time-based reality. When I tell him Jenny is stopping by in an hour, he will begin watching for her immediately, so I am careful not to mention a future plan or event until it is imminent.

Several days after our discussion about talking to God, and after going to what I thought would be a challenging appointment to have his ears cleaned, Ulf says, "I feel so good inside. I had asked God to be with me and He is. It really works!" I agree; it's better than meds.

Ulf often speaks of peace and being peaceful. This is a recorded transcript:

> I ask him the question: *"What does peace mean to you?"*
>
> Ulf responds: *"I think it has to do with living in peace, seeing your life in peace and sharing it with others and helping them to live that way."*
>
> I ask: *"How do you share peace?"*
>
> Ulf replies: *"Well, with the people we meet when we go out. I smile at them when they're not smiling. I want them to get a feeling for the energy and to allow that into their body, enjoy it and have some fun! You see, there's so much in there (touching his heart) so much energy we can share. If we have that kind of feeling ourselves, we have to share it because we can't use it all ourselves."*
>
> I say: *"Tell me about peace."*

Ulf says: *"The peace of God is the way to live. We know there are energies out there that can come to us and help us without our really knowing. It just comes through, you see. And it will be caught up in you. You will get it into you. It's your attitude, your way of doing, how you talk, how you look. And do you look like someone who is just having fun and want to share it? If you feel good, you'll pass that on. That's just a natural thing. And of course that book there, A Course in Miracles, has some of that same thing, which is written in a way that catches you and that you like and that you want to join it and work with it. And it doesn't have to take long."*

* * * * * * * * *

Ulf loves reading a book we recently received from Judy and Whit entitled "Peace," edited by Efrat Sar-Shalom Hanegbie. We met Efrat and Seffi, her husband, when they visited us in Sedona. Together they had founded "Zman Midbar," a spiritual ecological site for peace, located in the Judean desert, Israel. Efrat was part of the team that translated *A Course in Miracles* into Hebrew. Seffi and Ulf went to Bell Rock to meditate and sit quietly while taking in the expansive vistas. The memory of that quiet time has stayed with Ulf. *Peace* is a lovely book that uses select phrases from the *Course* about peace, a word that appears over seventeen hundred times! It places a phrase in the English *Course* between the Hebrew and Arabic translations. This message of peace expressed in the languages of common "enemies" is an extraordinary symbol of joining with God in peace.

This morning as we sat on the sofa holding hands, Ulf said, "Aren't we lucky to have this great loving energy between us. It makes everything so peaceful." We then read our books. For me, it is something light and humorous, while Ulf reads his new favorite book, *Peace*. It is amazing how this book so intently captures his full attention. Reading the short quotes on peace is easy for him to comprehend. Remembering that he met the author, who communicated with us, makes it very personal for him.

Ulf reads his new favorite book

17. PLAY TIME

*O*ne thing Ulf and I share is a sense of play, especially now that his "kid" is finding expression. I needed games to play with Ulf, since our outdoor adventures have been curtailed by the weather. We had just returned from Walgreen's where I bought a set of colored dominoes. I proceed to lay the dominoes out on the table and instruct him to match the numbers with the colored dots. At first he has difficulty discriminating differences, and then he slowly improves. Finally he laughs and says, "I am glad this isn't the only thing we have to do." So much for being the activities director! We play our version of a game until he wins, making it a little more interesting for him. When we play again later, I jokingly tell him that I was going to win even if I had to trick him. He laughs and says, "You are such a kid!"

Play can be very focused and intense for children. There is a sense of tapping into another energy that makes whatever they are doing so alive and in the moment. That is how I often feel with Ulf. Recently, I find myself so touched by this feeling that it brings tears to my eyes. My first thought is, am I depressed? In fact it is quite the opposite. It's difficult to describe. It is as if something is opening a part of my heart when we are just "being" together.

Our play can be fun and games or simply talking about God. It is the timelessness of these activities that puts them into another realm. Friends often ask if I miss our busy life—entertaining friends, going to movies, traveling. There is something about not *having* to do anything that has great appeal to me now and provides that open space. Ulf is more peaceful than I have ever seen him. There's a gentleness about him that resonates on a deep level when we are alone. At times, when we are with others, I can sense that he tries to "measure up." With me, he feels such acceptance that there is no need to search for a long-lost mask. It is the same when he is with our friends, Whit and Judy. After our last visit, he remarked for days about the energy he shared with them. To that, I replied, "It takes one to know one!"

When we were shopping recently, Ulf said to a tired looking couple with a child, "I bet she (the wife) is the real boss." The man smiled and agreed. Then Ulf said, "But I can see you love each other, so that's okay. Enjoy your time together." They both smiled broadly, as did others within earshot. When we walked away Ulf said, "See, that is what I like to do, make people feel better by making them smile." And that is how our shopping trips go, Ulf spreading good cheer. I try to take him some place every day where he can have an opportunity to share his sense of being playful and happy.

Touching that playful part of our selves is much more than just playing games. I want to bring Ulf the opportunity to experience the energy that the spontaneous nature of play generates, which is a sense of freedom from worry or concern. Playful energy is a memory that lingers with him and that he likes repeating. We had our playful moments before, but as with "time," Ulf is revisiting "play" in its simplest form. As in most creative endeavors, play brings our focus to the "present moment," where he now lives.

18. Forgiveness

A *Course in Miracles* says that forgiveness is the key to happiness, and that forgiving and receiving are one. It further says that by practicing forgiveness toward one whom you think of as an enemy (someone who irritates you), and one whom you consider a friend you learn to see them both as one. This has been a journey of patience and forgiveness for me. It is difficult for me to balance being in a timeless zone and still having to schedule appointments and know when to put out the garbage. When I am sharing Ulf's timeless space, he feels safe and happy. Those times when I am on the phone with a friend, or have a friend over for lunch and he hears the chattering, it is as if the energy field has shifted for him. It is the same when Ulf listens to programs showing violence on television—such as the news—which really reduces our options for watching! The energy visibly affects and upsets him, even though he cannot fully comprehend what is being said. Maybe whenever we leave the "present moment" and return to "time," Ulf senses that difference. When we are "in the moment," he is centered and alert.

For instance, several days ago, I went to my friend Shelley's office to have a much-needed therapeutic massage for my knee. I have known Shelley for many years and she has been there for me on many occasions during this time. While she was tending to me, Ulf had to stay in the waiting room. Twice during our session, Shelley had to leave and bring him back after he walked outside.

Later, at home, I say to him, "Your unwillingness to stay in the waiting room interrupted our session and that is not fair to me." I begin to cry. All the times when I did not feel supported or did not have my own needs met by Ulf begin to surface. Not specifics, but general feelings where those empty spaces—which probably exist in every relationship—awaken my emotional memories. He asks if my sadness has to do with what he did that day. I tell him, no, it's more about the past. Ulf immediately begins to respond in a loving and caring way. He says, "Those feelings have been there a long time and are way down. First, let them be there, and then release them. If a part of your ego is there, clean out the feeling and let it go. There is something that brings out our ego when we are unhappy; that happens all over the world." Needless to say, his insightful, supportive, compassionate tone gets my attention and my tears stop. A long period of silence passes between us. He turns to me and says, "Look at the fire in the fireplace and see how it burns things up. Think of your feelings and just let them burn up in the fire." He pauses and says," I don't know how, but that thought just came to my mind."

The word, "forgiveness" comes to *my* mind. Through Ulf's gentle guidance I do feel a lifting of heaviness from my heart, a heaviness that I did not even know existed. I was harboring guilt toward Ulf for this feeling of "lack" in myself. In that moment, it becomes clear that I need to forgive myself for my projection onto him. The *Course* says to forgive friend and enemy equally. We are then invited to merge the light we see in both of them. In the shared light that is reflected back to us, we become one. Ulf seems to embody these dualities for me at this time. His lesson is my lesson. Forgiveness is our key. Perhaps by seeing the wholeness and light reflected in him, I free myself. So I ask, which one of us is "demented?"

This evening I find a lovely note from Ulf that he wrote about two years ago.

BEVERLY,

TAKE A LOOK AND FEEL THE ENERGY. GOD WILL BE WITH YOU ALL DAY AND LONGER IF ASKED. HE IS AVAILABLE AS LONG AS YOU KEEP AN OPEN HEART!! Today is the day to see life with great GRATITUDE. Anytime you need support, I will be there for you. I may need to train myself a bit but My INTENTION is to be "THERE" FOR YOU.

LOVE,

YOUR HUSBAND,

ULF

19. It's About Love

*U*lf had a traumatic experience when the dentist put the squishy blue stuff used to make dental partial molds into his mouth. Although Ulf knew him, he was not clear about what he was doing. After a few minutes Ulf tried to take the stuff out of his mouth and get out of the chair. I managed to get him back in the chair, but Ulf was upset and embarrassed. When we got home, he called the office to apologize.

Before our second dental appointment, to pick up the partial, we stopped at a store. Walking in, we saw a bin of stuffed animals. One in particular caught Ulf's eye. He picked it up and said, "I really want this." He was holding a little brown teddy bear wearing a sweatshirt. Across the front of the sweatshirt was the word LOVE. Later, Ulf carried "Teddy" into the dental office, greeted the dentist with a smile, and said, "I brought this to tell you about love. Love is something you have to share." Naturally the dentist and others watching were touched.

Teddy has become Ulf's new best friend. He loves touching his forehead and feeling the softness of his fur. We are sitting on the sofa enjoying a quiet moment. Ulf is stroking Teddy's head when he asks me in a gentle, somewhat dreamy way, "How do we feel love?" I thought a moment and said, "When we open our hearts to love, it flows through us to everyone and everything, maybe even to Teddy." This got his attention. From that moment on, his relationship to Teddy took on new meaning. There followed gentle and soft "conversations" as he held Teddy.

Ulf with Teddy

Ulf understands that Teddy is a toy, yet uses it as a symbol of a concept he does not fully comprehend. None of us do. It is not as if he sees the world as a young child. I often observe him expressing himself in a spontaneous and uncomplicated way, yet with total awareness of what he is doing. There is an element of innocence in his desire to express the energy he has named Love.

Ulf expresses this innocence in his contacts with other people in a gentlemanly manner. One day we were walking along the path around Spring Lake where Ulf has an opportunity to greet people. As a couple in their mid thirties walk past us Ulf says, "You look very good together." They stop and turn around to see if he is talking about them. Ulf turns to the man and says, "It is important that you pay more attention to what she is saying." They both begin to laugh. She tells Ulf "This is our third date and that is exactly what we were discussing." Ulf then replies, "Smile more often so she knows you care." The woman suppresses a grin as they walk away, smiling, and in wonder at this gentleman who knows so much about them.

Continuing down the path, we notice a woman who we have seen on several trips to the park, sitting on a bench. She invites us to join her, so we sit down and begin to chat. She tells us that she has observed Ulf on previous visits to the park. She listens to Ulf and observes his kind manner, and tells him, "You're like the Dalai Lama!" Not remembering who she is referring to, but sensing that he must be a nice guy, Ulf smiles and says, "Thank you."

Another day Ulf says, "Let's go to that place where we have so much fun." I ask, "Spring Lake?" "No," he says, "it's where we go to get things to eat." Somewhat surprised, I say, "Safeway?" He says "Yes, that's the place!" He is able to speak to at least ten people on every trip, such as the older lady he sees who is looking a little downcast, pushing her cart along. Ulf stops in front of her and says, "My, that color looks so good on you." She sparks up, smiles and says "Thank you so much." He grins at her and says, "You have a lovely smile." As we walk away Ulf says, "See, I did it again. Make someone smile and be happy." I might add that Ulf is quite a handsome, well presented man who could elicit a smile from any woman. If he sees someone physically struggling, he'll say, "I hope you are better soon," and he always gets a surprised, "Thank you" in response. Some of these people are invisible to most of us. Ulf is very conscious of what he is doing, but what he does is done with such an open heart that no one notices or cares that he, himself, is "challenged." As we drive away he always says, "I feel so good and this energy just flows out of me."

Learning from the children I worked with, I have come to believe that we lose touch with our "Innocence" very early in life. Perhaps our interpretation of the Innocence of very young children has to do with witnessing our Spirit before it is contaminated by fear. What if Ulf is going through a *de*contamination process in which glimpses of that original joining with Innocence in Spirit is occurring? We might even call it glimpses into Love, which, by its very nature is then shared. Soon it will be Valentine's Day, the *one* day designated for "love." Maybe we could be inspired to extend that Innocence within ourselves and touch others with that Love *every* day! I think that is what Ulf, in his Innocence, is teaching. The *Course* says, "Teach only love for that is what you are."

Recording transcript:

One day, sitting together on the sofa and being warmed by the dancing flames in the fireplace, Ulf looks at me and my recorder captures him saying:

> *"One thing we have—let me take your hand—we love each other. And there is a strong energy that comes from that. Others may talk about Love but we live with Love. That's our life. You and I truly love each other and we show it many times."*

> I say, *"So you feel that love is the most important thing?"*

> *"Right. Initially we may not have it exactly the way we think it should be. I think the heart is a very good source to think of. We have love in both of our bodies, lots of love and we feel it in our hearts.*

That is Love speaking.

20. What is Death?

*W*e are still a month away from spring, so the bedroom is a little chilly. As I slowly open my eyes and reach for Ulf's hand, I notice that he is staring intently at the ceiling, deep in thought. I gently ask him, "What are you thinking about?" In a quiet voice he says, "I don't want to talk about it." As I softly encourage him he finally says, "The past and the future." Turning my body toward him and raising my head, I ask, "What are you thinking about the past?" Still looking at the ceiling, and sounding a little melancholy, he responds, "When I had things to do like help people in my business and had friends and family. Now I have no one and all I can do alone is walk around the outside of our house. If I go any farther I'll get lost. No one calls or cares anymore."

The honest recognition of his situation sinks into my head and brings me fully awake as I say, "What you are feeling is shared by lots of people as we grow older. You were more independent then and you must really miss that." We were silent for a while and then I ask, "What are you thinking about the future?" He said, in a quiet tone of resignation, "Dying. I feel like I'm dying. There is nothing left." I suggest gently, "Just accept whatever you are feeling and let it be." Ulf takes a deep breath and I say, "Close your eyes and see if you can sense your spirit." He says, "I think it is inside me now," to which I add, "We are spirit and our spirit never dies. So I guess thoughts of death come when we forget we are spirit."

For Ulf, forgetting his past and losing his independence is like death. We all experience forms of death repeatedly throughout our lives with every loss, every change, and every fleeting moment. When we struggle against those thought forms that are slowly evaporating, we suffer. I see Ulf struggling between gracefully letting go and fighting to maintain some portion of his life and who he thought he was.

One of my favorite parts in the *Course* is called "The Little Garden" which states: "The body is a tiny fence around a little part of a glorious and complete idea. It draws a circle, infinitely small, around a very little segment of Heaven, splintered from the whole, proclaiming that within it is your kingdom where God can enter not…. The Thought of God surrounds your little kingdom…. See how life springs up everywhere. The desert becomes a garden, green and deep and quiet, offering rest to those who lost their way and wander in the dust."

In an enthusiastic voice I say, "Let's get dressed and see what is in our life *now!*" Just as enthusiastically, Ulf jumps out of bed saying, "Let's go!" We eat some breakfast and head toward Spring Lake. Usually there are lots of animals and people for Ulf to share a friendly "hello, have a nice day." It is the middle of the week and the path around the lake is very quiet. We rest on a bench near a small inlet of water where ducks come to feed at the edge of the lake. We sit in silence and watch. The sky and clouds paint a lovely backdrop to the shimmering lake where several small sailboats meander. Buds and little blossoms are beginning to bring the trees and bushes to life. There is an aliveness in the quiet hush of nature. After a while Ulf says, "God must be around. It's so peaceful."

This experience was a contrast to his earlier thoughts about loss and dying. It is this difference in our contracted versus our expanded experience that seems to define our struggle to be free. Death could be defined as our lack of awareness of the presence of love and peace in our life.

In the "Little Garden" we are asked to invite love to enter into our bleak and joyless kingdom and to transform it into a garden of peace and welcome. It seems we have found that garden, at least for a little while.

21. Letting Go of Anger

*U*lf slams his fist onto the table and shouts in a loud voice, "What is wrong with me? Something is wrong with me! What have I done wrong?" "Why don't you ask God?" I reply. He turns to me with real intensity in his eyes and says, "God can go to hell! He doesn't talk to me anymore!" I suggest that maybe he could not hear Him because he is shouting.

This seemed to encapsulate a series of incidences in which Ulf responds in an agitated and aggressive manner to benign situations. I am aware that the progressive damage to the brain can produce these unusual responses, but Ulf has never been aggressive. He is aware of the inappropriateness of his behavior and later castigates himself. It is difficult for me to observe this painful litany that expresses the escalation of his frustration. Ulf is not fantasizing about his situation. He is unable to initiate an activity or be self-motivated. He sits at his desk, looking serious and shuffling papers to look busy, surely trying to emulate his life before his illness.

Last week I pulled a book from the shelf for him to look at: *Love is Letting Go of Fear*. It was written by our friend Jerry Jampolsky in the late 70's and is based on *A Course in Miracles*. I thought it would be helpful to Ulf at this time. The book has simply written sections like "I'm Never Upset for the Reason I think" and "I Can Escape the World I See by Giving up Attack Thoughts." Ulf likes to hold the book and carry it around. Something more than the words is resonating with him.

It has been said that anger is a defense mechanism masking fear. There seems to be more "power" in the energy of anger than in the expression of fear when we often feel power*less*. Much earlier, when Ulf would express anger in a joking way I would have him exaggerate the feeling to emphasize how "powerful" it made him feel. Again, Ulf rarely expressed anger directly. I would then say, "When you are angry, the ego is in charge, not you. It is your choice to decide if you want to express God or your ego." Using the word "ego" in this simple way made it clear to Ulf that he was at least in charge of how he wanted to feel.

This is new territory for me, but I am aware that medications can be helpful when Ulf can no longer control these feelings. I am in touch with doctors about this, but there do not seem to be many alternatives to heavy-duty drugs, so I am hesitant to go down that road. By now, you'd think there would be less intrusive options. Prescribing pills, with Ulf's diagnosis, becomes a one-size-fits-all management approach. Ulf is truly suffering during this part of his unraveling process. He knows he is not this person, and is over-whelmed by these feelings. As I said earlier regarding death, this is a dying process for him.

After all we have been through, this journey with Ulf begins to shed some light on my own hidden defense system. If we indeed cre-ate our own reality, what have I created here and how do I respond to everything that is happening? I do not walk on eggshells for Ulf. I express my emotions fully (and, I admit, not always appropriately). As a result, I have learned how to release my attachment to those emotions that have kept me "safe" all my life. That's what defenses pretend to do. Fear and uncertainty are core beliefs that we try not to feel. It is easier to keep those feelings hidden and attack someone else.

All of this reminds me of being in Hawaii in the late 70's and meeting a Kahuna named Morrnah Simeona, and her associate Dr. Hew Len. They taught an ancient Hawaiian healing art called the Ho'oponopono. This ancient art says that we create everything in our path, and by owning that creation, we can change our experience.

I attended a gathering at which Dr. Len, a psychologist, told a story about when he was placed in charge of the "lockup" unit at a hospital psychiatric ward where some of the patients had become so unruly that they were placed in chains. Dr. Len introduced his staff to a system of being with the patients, not as different and superior, but as equals on their journey. After a while the ward became so quiet and peaceful that chains were no longer needed. The administrators were puzzled as to what had transpired but no one shared the "secret" because it would have been regarded as "witchcraft." Dr. Len told many such stories which opened our minds to the possibilities of freeing ourselves.

This now is my challenge in learning about my own unraveling process. My focus has been on Ulf for so long that I have neglected to witness my own lessons. I have now begun to more keenly observe my reactions to this stressful and heart-wrenching path I have chosen to be on, watchful for whatever lessons await me.

Oh, what mysteries our fears hide! As Jerry's book says, "We find love when we let go of fear." We defend against this invisible curtain so much, we must be afraid of love. What a miracle it would be if Ulf could get to the other side of his fear and find the peace and love he is so desperately seeking. I believe this is the miracle waiting for all of us.

22. GOD WHO?

There is a lovely Day Club in our area for seniors who no longer can function totally alone. The facility is called Primrose. There is a large protected outside area with paved walks lined with flowers, along a manicured lawn. The attractive one-story facility also houses permanent and temporary residents, but it is not a nursing home. They have music, dancing and a very relaxed, welcoming environment. After talking with the staff, I decided it would be a good place for Ulf to spend a few hours and give me some respite. Another objective was to have a place where he could go if I became ill. (Another step in planning ahead for unknown tomorrows!)

The first day, as we casually walk along the path, Ulf wants to know why he is here with all those "old people," some in wheelchairs. I suggest to him that he is here to help these people by making them smile and feel good about themselves. By doing this, he is also helping God by sharing his energy. That pleases him.

Later, I observed Ulf approach a well-dressed woman in a wheelchair who had lost her ability for facial expression. I thought, "Oh my, is Ulf going to try and get her to smile?" He said these extremely insightful words to her: "I know you are smiling inside." Her eyes danced as she realized someone had finally noticed.

After he's had a successful day at Primrose helping all those "old people," I tell Ulf that God must be very happy with him and appreciates the help. Ulf says, "You really think so? What's God's last name so I can look up his phone number and give him a call?" That question throws me, but I manage to say, "God is not like a person with an office. God is everywhere and in everything." Ulf has a hard time with that one, saying, "Like in the air?" He wants to talk with Him "man to man," like doing business together. Hey, maybe that is what is happening, they are running a business!

While talking with my friend Fay Richards, who lives in Sedona, I mention Ulf's comments and questions about God. Fay and I have had numerous conversations about metaphysics. She told me about her "beyond death" experience, when she was given the revelation that we come here with much more knowledge than what we are aware of. She said, "When one is in a period of timelessness, that person is given an expanded consciousness of the oneness of all living things, and even of the inanimate." Fay is following my stories about Ulf, so she shares a story about her daughter. I ask her to write it and send it to me. She writes: "When Vali was about four years old, she told me she had heard about something called "god," and asked what it is. Since I don't do religion, I told her God was what lives inside of everything that is. She asked, "Can we see it?" I said, "Perhaps, if you really look for it." Later, she came running into the house and with breathless excitement announced, "I just found where God lives!" We raced to our sunny Florida backyard and she pointed to a young banana plant. "Here, look!" Truly, there was, at the base of the concentric leaves, a magical golden-green light that glowed when viewed from above. "Yes," I said, "That's what God can look like."

Now try to imagine someone like Ulf, who might as well have just arrived on this planet, trying to understand a non-physical, abstract concept like "God." It has been a challenge to attempt to explain the concept of God to one who still does not understand why he cannot just phone him. I have enlisted "God" to travel with me on this journey. My concept of God, however, is probably more of the "other dimensional" variety than the one with a face, which would denote a human being, something familiar that Ulf could understand. Ulf explains, "God is the loving feeling I have that I want to share with others. That is what happens when you invite God's energy to join your energy." In listening to Ulf, I have come to realize that, to him, God and Love are interchangeable expressions of gentleness and sharing. He even sees God in Teddy.

We often use words automatically without realizing what their real meaning is to us, especially words like God, Death, Love, Heaven, Hell, Eternity, plus many other words, which have been used in an effort to explain something we do not remotely understand. We know that when we die, we are not "alive" and do not move around anymore. We know that love seems to come and go.

In some religious cultures, God is judgmental, punitive, vengeful and demanding of our allegiance. He is described as a man with a long gray beard who is all-knowing and powerful. In other cultures, the sun represents his power. The Greeks had mythological gods. Every culture has a symbol that represents something more powerful than humans, probably because we can look up at the sky and at the horizon and figure out that there is something going on that is larger than we are. As human beings, we often use our bodies to create the illusion of power that can result in the age-old conflict of opposition to others, either individually or collectively, in war. The degree of opposition is irrelevant. It all has the same purpose—separation. The creation of a false power, or "god," is what can block our experience of a gentle, loving God. The *Course* says, "The memory of God comes to the quiet mind. It cannot come where there is conflict, for a mind at war against itself remembers not eternal gentleness."

The fact that Ulf, in this twist of fate, has become a stranger to himself is a reminder to all of us of the impermanence of our identity and the confusion that follows as our perception of ourselves changes. So now it is not only, "Who is God," but "Who am I?" Whatever prior relationship Ulf had with God has changed because *he* has changed and this has created confusion. Since these concepts have been and are very vital to him, I try to keep my comments to him simple. At the same time, he seems to have an instinctive, non-verbal grasp of these words.

So I guess it all comes down to belief. I can believe anything is true for me, but that may not make it true for you. For instance, if I had a "near death experience" or was beamed up onto a space ship, and someone told me that did not happen, I would be more than a little put off. We can have a direct experience that reinforces the belief in what is true for each of us. Belief, whether conscious or unconscious, positive or negative, can ultimately determine our own experience. The *Course* says that in God's vision we are all One, joined and connected. Isn't this all about reconnecting with something from which we only *imagined* we were ever *disconnected*? Hey, I think I'm on to something! Maybe I should tell Ulf that God's last name is Hamilton and they are somehow related!

23. Who Are You?

*A*bout a week later, as I walked into the Day Club to pick up Ulf, he asked, "Who are *you* and where is my wife I have loved for many years? She's coming to get me." I said, "I'm your wife! I brought you here today." He said, "No you're not." I left the room, emerging several minutes later with a big smile saying, "Sorry I'm late. I'm here to pick you up." Ulf said, "Oh, I'm *so* glad to see you!" This confusion with facial recognition often occurs when a person with cognitive disabilities is in an environment with many other faces and has difficulty distinguishing one from another.

This confusion also signals the beginning of Ulf's inability to maintain emotional stability. He continues to show more confusion, such as when he says, "I need to go home," when he's already home. It is sad to witness this increasing disconnect with his surroundings. The doctor is trying some medication. I told him, after a week, that it had a negative effect on Ulf, so he doubled the dose! That does not make sense to me. I am at a loss to know where this is headed. It seems to me Ulf is probably having more small strokes.

Later, at home, after not recognizing me when I pick him up at Day Club, he continues asking when Beverly is coming from Texas. I try to "lighten it up" by saying, "You're acting like you have a harem, with one lady here feeding you, one driving you from Day Club and another who is on her way here from Texas. I wish you did have a harem, but I hate to disappoint you, I'm it!!" He does respond to the humor, so I know what to do. I bring out the photo album and begin to realize, as we look at the photos, that I *do* look different. It has been a long time since I took a close look at myself in the mirror. No wonder he is waiting for "her" to show up and replace this old lady!

I finally give him a mild sedative. He calms down and says, "Let's forget all that. You're here, I'm here, we have a lovely house and car and that is all that matters." Just then, we look out the window and there is a rainbow emerging from the hills right in front of us. Excitedly I say, "Look at that beautiful rainbow!" Ulf looks at it and remarks, "Maybe that's God saying hello." I am grateful for the subject change. Thanks, God!

Ulf opens his *Peace* book and reads to me for about forty minutes. We then talk about how, when he is peaceful, he and God can work together to help those "old people" at the Day Club.

Our friends, Haizen and Max, have put Ulf and me on the Unity Prayer list. I called their prayer line and a lovely person spoke beautiful, inspiring words in a very gentle voice. I really needed that. As you can imagine, this is not easy and I feel very much alone. Looking back from where we are now, I can see Ulf's need to become closer to God. That may be where he is headed.

24. I NEED DO NOTHING

"I Need Do Nothing" is another one of my favorite sections in the *Course* and probably the most difficult to practice in times of stress. This past week, however, Ulf made me a "true believer." I made arrangements for him to spend respite time, overnight, at Primrose. As we prepare to go to the initial intake meeting with the staff, Ulf begins having a drug reaction and is in the process of having a meltdown experience. He becomes more confused and wants to leave the house to go "home." I call Haizen to talk with him and that has a quieting effect on Ulf. To distract him, I dish up some ice cream and we talk about his conversation with Haizen. He settles down and we drive to Primrose, arriving early for the intake. We take a leisurely walk around the grounds and sit at a table outside. Someone brings lunch to us in this very lovely, warm setting. Ulf likes the staff and they share that affection, so he feels comfortable here and seems peaceful now. I stand up to take him into the Day Club building so I can attend the intake meeting, but Ulf cannot stand up alone. Finally, with help, he is guided inside while I go to the meeting. After observing him, they say that because they are not a medical facility, they cannot take him until the physical problem has been diagnosed and suggest we go to the Kaiser Hospital Emergency Room.

After being admitted to the ER, Ulf is medicated and restrained with straps. It's painful for me to observe this enforced captivity.

While still in the ER, Ulf is confused and wonders why this is happening. I briefly leave the room and when I return he is relaxed and I smile at him. In his altered state he said, "You have a reason to be sad." How did he know I had gone to the restroom to cry?

After being sedated for four hours in the ER, he is admitted to the hospital. They begin assessing the drug he had been prescribed. I am told that when he is stabilized he will be transferred to a facility where he will spend a couple of weeks to secure his medication. Then, hopefully, he will return home. Who knows for sure? I cannot bear the thought of us not being together, so have begun to investigate facilities where we both can live.

I have not a clue what is coming. All I know is that this is an incredible journey of love. If there are tears on this page, you know why. However, in spite of the trauma, this is a beneficial path for Ulf. He now has a group of professional people assessing him because of the physical manifestation of briefly not being able to walk steadily—a result of the drug. There is no immediate plan to discharge him from the hospital.

The section in the *Course*, "I need do nothing" states in part, "At no single instant does the body exist at all. It is always remembered or anticipated, but never experienced just *now*. Only its past and future make it seem real. Time controls it entirely.... To do nothing is to rest, and make a place within you where the activity of the body ceases to demand attention.... Yet there will always be this place of rest to which you can return.... This quiet center, in which you do nothing, will remain with you."

This passage reminds me of Ulf's fascination with the "present moment." Maybe that is the space in which we join with formlessness and timelessness where the body has no meaning, even for an instant. I believe Ulf and I often share that space by not "doing" anything to achieve it, just surrendering to the moment.

This has been a journey of our return to Innocence. It has brought me full circle to what I wrote years ago in my book *Grains of Sand*: "Innocence is born into the dream." In a strange way, Ulf is awakening from the dream and is "Flowering in the fragrance of love." As that love surrounds Ulf and me, in the present moment, I know I need do nothing.

25. It Is Here, Now

*I*n the journey I now find myself taking I'm always exploring new territory, much as my great-grandparents did when pioneering the West in a covered wagon.

My travel adventures and spiritual curiosity have in some aspects prepared me for this unchartered path Ulf and I are traveling together. There is something about being in unknown territory, out of the ruts we create to feel secure, that heightens our awareness. I find this energizing. However, traversing the terrain of Ulf's diagnosis and treatment options is not a place I would consider visiting again.

When Ulf and I explored this path through meditation and other maps that guided us, we learned that the journey was more inward than outwardly directed. It was interesting for me to observe Ulf resonating to this inward exploration as he read and wrote about this quiet experience. There is an element of familiarity about this practice that gives him comfort and is now his ever-present guide as his past disappears. At this time in my life with Ulf, I am learning, bit by bit, to be at peace with the impermanence of life. Writing about our journey as it unfolds has a way of opening me to another level of consciousness where time simply goes away.

The other day I was talking on the phone and looking at the view outside the window, when I became aware of a small tree, full of pink blossoms. I had been looking right at it the whole time but did not "see" it. The *Course* says, "We look neither ahead nor backwards. We look straight into the present." My biggest lesson thus far is the knowing that life—"It"—is always here, now, when viewed through the eyes of love.

I visit Ulf in the hospital at least three times a day. This particular day is good for him with his sense of humor showing through as we joust back and forth about all the lovely ladies serving him. After giving him some water and cookies, I just sit there holding his hand. Liz, a petite Nurse's Aide from Africa, enters the room. Ulf looks at her and smiles. He says, "Do you know God loves you?" He continues, "God knows people and knows what a wonderful person you are and how helpful you are to others." For the first time since arriving at the hospital he begins to cry. He then puts his hand over his heart, gestures outward and says, "I am so grateful to God who has brought these kind people to help me." He is expressing himself in a soft and mellow voice. I leave the room briefly to speak with the social worker. When I return, Liz is singing "Amazing Grace" to Ulf. There is a hush in the room except for her singing. I feel this loving energy mixing with the soft sunlight bathing the scene. Whatever else happens, in that moment Love in all its purity touches everyone there. In this precious, present moment, Ulf is showing us that Love extends far beyond the condition of his body. In his simple way, he is telling me that when he leaves his body, he will always be Here, Now... nothing really changes.

26. Space Between the Dots

*U*lf is transferred from the hospital to The Oaks, a facility much better staffed for his recovery and stabilization. I check into a motel to be close by. Eric arrives from Japan on business and visits his dad several times. He is being very helpful to me as an advocate, talking with the Oaks Director, who is very available and hands-on with his patients. Eric and I also have some nice, long, thoughtful lunches, giving me a respite, for which I am thankful. This is a sad time for Eric. He has to return to Japan and does not know if he will see his father again. Jenny joins us in these hospital moves, and is a comfort to me. Her time is filled with three young children and many animals, but she does what she can to be there for us.

Having to move around to be close to Ulf has put me in survival mode. I am not allowing my feelings and emotions to the surface, even to have a good cry. After a week at The Oaks, Ulf's condition rapidly deteriorates. The Director and doctor call me into the office and tell me Ulf is ill and they are going to transfer him back to the hospital. I check out of the motel and into another one, close to yet another hospital, where I am soon asked to join the hospital counselors in a meeting. We are sitting in a comfortably furnished room, getting acquainted, when the doctor comes in. He says Ulf contracted an infection while in the hospital and may not survive. He asks, compassionately, did I want him on life support? The counselors say they will respect my wishes. I say to them, "It is not my wish but Ulf's they need to respect, and his wish is to not go on life support. He has signed papers to that effect." After I make that statement, they each tell me how difficult it is for people they counsel to "let go" of their loved ones. I reply that it's *because* I love him, that I want him to go in peace. They share with me how refreshing it is to hear me make such a clear statement after seeing so much suffering by those who choose otherwise. With my permission, they transfer Ulf to a hospice facility. Again, I follow the ambulance and dare anyone on the road to come between us, which tells me that some emotions are beginning to surface. However, something also tells me that if I open the door to my feelings even a crack, I will fall apart.

I check into a motel next door to Ulf's facility and rush over to see him. He soon responds to the doses of morphine he is given in the likelihood that he is in pain. I sit quietly and hold his hand. It is one of the few quiet times I have had with him since this medical ordeal began, giving me the space to become aware of the emotional pain that is just below the surface. I know it is there because it has a tight grip on my chest but I am not prepared to bring it up. After being with Ulf a while, I pick up some food and return to my motel room. At this moment, I am doing what brings me peace, writing.

We rarely question the space between our bodies and objects such as a chair, table or other bodies. If these zillions of pixel dots, like the flowers, the trees, the birds and the bees and our bodies that define our physical reality disappear, we call it "death." That is Ulf's experience at this moment. There is no "him" or any object he perceives. There is no "time" to measure past, future or distance. He is currently suspended in a space, without "dots" to identity as a chair or a tree. There is no labeling of these dots, or judgments of them as good dots or bad dots. *There are no dots.* Maybe that is called Heaven! Don't we have wonderful imaginations? Have we used these "dots" to create the illusion of separate parts to a larger whole that we never in fact left? These dots appear to obstruct our awareness of this larger universe where we are all joined. Is Ulf simply vaporizing what he created in order to have this experience? If so, maybe he is just returning to his home, the one without all the dots, the one where his friend, God, lives.

As long as you are here dearest Ulf, I will hold your hand with love.

27. I AM SPIRIT

*I*t is after midnight when I finish writing *Space Between the Dots.* Strangely, I feel very good. There is a surge of energy flowing through me. I sink into a big comfortable chair and think about what I have written, even looking around the room at all the "dots" called "furniture." I have my nightgown on and am ready for bed, when a voice from inside me says, "Decide what clothes you want to wear when they call." Suddenly, I have a very strong feeling that Ulf is leaving his body. Instantly I realize that the energy I am feeling is the energy we shared, and it is coming from Ulf. With trembling hands, I immediately throw on some clothes and run next door to the nursing home to be with Ulf. I enter the building and begin walking down the hall and see the attendants leaving his room. They tell me he has just "gone." Ulf has left his body on his birthday to become a Spirit. I sit next to him and hold his hand.

A Course in Miracles says, "I am not a body, I am free. For I am still as God created me." Ulf is now free to fill the space with Love instead of "dots." This has been a journey of love for me and will continue to be.

Rest in that Peace Ulf, which you so dearly Love.

PART III

Lessons in Love from Spirit

1. LIFE AFTER "LIFE"

*W*hen Ulf began to decline, I became aware of the necessity of releasing him from my need for him to remain here. This was now his personal journey. Many people "hang on" because loved ones are not willing to let them go. This is something the counselors at the hospital had observed. I wanted Ulf to be totally free to do whatever he chooses, and for him to know that I would be at peace with that decision.

As I say in I am Spirit, I felt a surge of energy flow through me just as I finished writing that night. This unexpected reaction to Ulf leaving his body continues to puzzle me. It is a different feeling from relief or letting go. It began before I knew Ulf had gone... in fact it coincided with the time he left.

Driving home a few hours later, I find myself thinking that we have been through so many changes in how we related, maybe this will be just one more new step to learn in that dance. I feel so expansive it is as if Ulf is beaming like a 1000-watt bulb saying "Hi Bev." I arrive home, unload the car from days of staying at motels, not thinking about much of anything. All of a sudden I "hear," "I know what you've been doing! I now know about your writing!" I hadn't told Ulf about my writing because I didn't want him to be self-conscious. The realization of what that thought means hits me and I begin to laugh so hard tears roll down my cheeks. I wonder if this is our new way of communicating.

I am open to anything "other worldly" if it is revealed in a natural, gentle way. No drama for me in that category! The evening after Ulf left, I have dinner with Linda who initiated my writing. Driving home, my "intuition"—or inner voice—says to me, "Do not go that way" (the one lined with overhanging trees), so I make a jog to the other road. My curiosity is beginning to peak in regard to these instructions I'm following. As I pass Walgreens I scan the aisles in my mind, thinking that maybe I am to pick something up there. Nothing comes to mind, so I continue driving. I drive along for a few more minutes, still puzzled, when suddenly I come to the top of a hill and see the most incredible full moon in a clear sky such as I never have seen before. I drive toward it all the way home. I would have never seen such a sight if I had taken the other road, due to the heavy overhead branches of trees. The full moon was one of Ulf's favorite things in the sky. He had spoken about being there, and, when returning to Earth, seeing us all as one, much as some astronauts described. Maybe the moon is Ulf's way of reminding me that he's still around. We actually do live in the Valley of the Moon. What a lovely gift!

The *Course* says, "It is quite possible to reach God. In fact it is very easy, because it is the most natural thing in the world.... The way will be open if you believe it is possible." I guess we all can join you, Ulf, where you are now. There is really nothing separating any of us from that expanded, infinite, loving, space you now call "home," except our thinking it is someplace else, and we are someone else. You are right here, right now, and the same Spirit you always were. Maybe there's just one less "dot" you used to call "life." There is only one Life.

2. Beyond All Idols

*E*very morning since Ulf's "re-birthday," when I am in that blurry space between waking and sleeping, the thought "he's gone" jolts me awake. That realization opens a feeling of grief, which is an intense feeling. I begin to bring a certain kind of awareness to the feeling moving through me. As I pay attention, I notice that the emotion though attached to my present loss, resonates throughout my past. It already existed before Ulf left. I am projecting a well-established emotion onto my current situation. We forget or perhaps it is that we are unaware of a cellular encoding in our emotional memory that is always searching for expression.

What was generating this response in me? Was Ulf my "idol" that I thought would complete me but now is no longer present? The holes within our psyche that we use people and objects to fill for completion are central to the idea of separation from the wholeness of who we really are. Earlier, as Ulf was "leaving," I was writing about the "dots," which represent physical form of any kind. We can see them as blocks, deflecting, and distorting the light, like a lampshade or we can see the light shining through them. When we attach emotional significance to a dot, it becomes a symbol of our projected emptiness, without which we feel incomplete.

As I am pondering these thoughts, I ask Ulf's spirit to guide me. I reach for the *Course*, which is in front of me, and aimlessly open to the chapter, "Beyond All Idols." These words immediately catch my eye: "Behind the search for every idol lies the yearning for completion. Wholeness has no form because it is unlimited. To seek a special person or a thing to add to you to make yourself complete can only mean that you believe some form is missing. And by finding this, you will achieve completion in a form you like. This is the purpose of an idol; that you will not look beyond it, to the source of the belief that you are incomplete."

The word "forgiveness" fills my very being. I realize my desire to "forgive" myself as well as Ulf for any misplaced energy that speaks to our incompleteness. In those areas where we think the other completes us, our awareness of oneness is blocked. There are no dots or idols where Ulf is now. I would not have my thoughts of being made incomplete by his leaving keep us separate, and keep him trapped in my mind as a "false idol." As I did when he began losing his memory and I joined him in his "present moment," I now want to join him with the thought of being "whole" again.

The *Course* further states, "The light has come.... It has replaced the darkness" (idols and dots). The light in you is all that I would see, Ulf. I am so grateful for this journey without distance that we continue to share.

3. OVER THE RAINBOW

*E*xperience has a way of keeping me honest. It's one thing to talk about other dimensions, holographic universes, energy fields, near-death experiences, and "we're not a body," but it is another thing when someone you have been close to daily for many years no longer occupies a space you can see or where you can reach out and touch his hand. That condition has been labeled "Death," a word that ceases to have a negative or fearful meaning for me. As I wrote earlier, my "conversation" with Death three days before I actually faced the possibility of dying minimized any fear I had of Death. In fact, leaving my body then seemed like just another adventure.

However, Ulf leaving his body is giving me a much different perspective of that experience. I want to know how and where he is. It's like being left in a void of not "knowing." For me, having a personal experience is much easier than wondering what is happening to someone I love. I can better understand the tendency to wrap this "unknown" in religious mythology and weave countless stories fantasizing the probabilities, some of them fearful.

The journey is also a lonely one. Ulf seemed to be aware of people who were alone and appeared lonely. He would gently approach them and offer help or a kind word. In "day care" he extended his energy to the people trapped in wheel chairs and, for a moment, they didn't feel alone. I miss Ulf, "pimples" and all.

This is what happens in special relationships: You identify your body with another body. It is the human condition, the trump card of the ego, if you will. I have a card up my sleeve, however. That card is the energy I feel much of the time, which makes me want to connect with others and laugh. When I "remember not to laugh" I know I have lost the connection to my Source. I've unplugged the lamp. It's not energy concocted to override the sadness, but energy that allows my body to serve another purpose. It is my choice.

It also gives me comfort at this time to personify the energy connection with Ulf. There's a lot I do not know, or even pretend to know, but one thing I know for sure is that Ulf is happy and, as the *Course* says, "I'm not a body. I am free. I am as God created me." That is true in or out of our bodies. It's not the exclusive domain of those no longer occupying their bodies. So Ulf, let's meet at that playground where our free Souls go to play. I think it's somewhere over the rainbow.

4. THE BUTTERFLY WAY

*W*henever I wake up and see the hills covered in a heavy mist, which seems to bring a hush to the valley, I hurry to the kitchen. I then proceed to make tea and toast, pick up a book, set up the bed tray, and return to bed. It gives me a wonderful "snuggly" feeling that I call "cocooning."

On this particular day, like so many others, I read, cry, meditate, and in general get to know myself again. It has been a while since I could quietly look within for any length of time. What a luxury to pay no attention to time, to shut the world out and open to the space within me. How have I changed on this journey? Who was the "I" who had participated with Ulf in his "present moment"? The things that used to delight me, like visiting with friends or dinners full of conversation and laughter, time alone, were no longer a part of my landscape. Aspects of my previous identity no longer existed during this experience. I am also learning about different parts of myself that had not been fully expressed before Ulf took this detour out of time. Through Ulf's eyes I began to notice the finer, subtle aspects of nature he would point out on our walks. Strangers became friends, if even for a fleeting moment. Time somehow blurred, as the necessity of staying in the moment became my reality. How I had perceived this reality began to shift as the force of energy that flowed in this new way swept our past away.

Looking out the window at the hills peeking through the mist, this timeless feeling returns in the midst of tending to the many details since Ulf left. In bringing images of him to my mind, there is confusion. The person I knew for years went through many changes. I am inclined to look for something "constant" in what we had known from our past. When I attempt to retrieve those memories, however, I find that it is a moving kaleidoscope of images. I've become accustomed to the experience of Ulf's presence in the form of the energy we often shared. In my mind, I sense the loving, peaceful person he had been, minus any struggle or confusion. He is whole. This describes my current "present moment" when I think of Ulf.

The weather, like me, is changing. The sun is shining daily now and the mist has faded. I am now sipping my tea in the comfort of Ulf's favorite chair. I am aware of silently asking, even in making simple decisions, "which is the easiest one?" Not that one decision is more valid than the next but the exercise in awareness shows me that I am not alone. When I do feel alone, it is my focus that has changed. The energy of unity is within me; I do not have to go looking for it or wonder where it went.

Butterflies emerge from their cocoon and so do I, shedding one layer at a time. That wonderful feeling of "Lightness of Being" occurs in those moments. I call stopping to smell the flowers "the Butterfly Way."

5. Gifts from the Heart

*A*fter the day when I was "told" to take a different route home and was led to where I saw a huge moon right in front of me, I became more attentive to other interesting coincidences as they occurred.

One day a doe came into the space between the house and the fenced rose garden. In a light-handed manner, I thought I'd practice communicating with Ulf. Since he loved animals, maybe his energy could manifest through the deer. I became very still and focused on sending energy from my heart to the deer. To my surprise, the doe froze in her tracks, looked in my direction, and stayed in that position for over thirty minutes. I imagined stroking her, much like Ulf stroked his "love" bear. She eventually turned and quietly walked away. She now brings her two fawns to visit. They even lie down and curl up for a rest. They feel very peaceful and safe. Yesterday morning, I opened the blinds to see her sleeping, her head resting on her leg. Whenever she shows up, I think of Ulf.

There are many ways to open our hearts to the unknown. Ulf always felt at home in the energy of peace which is why he was so comfortable in nature and with animals. As I have explored the ways to continue our connection, I am most open when I experience that peaceful energy Ulf would mention whenever he took my hand. We may not be able to hold hands but we can share the space in-between our forms where I imagine he now presides. So I look for those moments when I become aware that I'm not alone.

The most memorable moment comes on the third month anniversary of Ulf's "birthday." Knowing it is "that" time, I go outside and see a beautiful full moon in a clear sky. I take these photos and, much to my surprise, when I download to my computer, I receive yet another gift from the heart! Out of four "normal" moon photos, taken seconds apart, one is in the shape of a heart. It is Ulf saying, "Hi," again.

Gift from Ulf's heart

6. LOVE SPEAKS

One of the things I miss about Ulf not being here are the affection and the expressions of love that he brought into my life. I'm feeling a little emotionally bankrupt these days. The first weeks in August can be defined primarily by feeling disconnected from the love within myself. I feel depressed, which is one of the many emotions of grief. My body is joining in this disconnect with little infections, antibiotics, and threats of yucky procedures. I am also questioning whether I could have done something different to change the outcome with Ulf. It appears to me that I'm beating up on myself. Yet another layer is being exposed.

Like all the emotions that have surfaced since the loss of Ulf's loving presence, I just accept them and wear them like a tattered old coat, even though it is very disquieting and uncomfortable. I have discovered that by letting these unwelcome feelings be what they are, they begin to fade on their own. These unloving feelings will certainly revisit me on occasion, but those visits will get shorter and shorter. Some people say that these unwanted feelings, which disconnect us from our spirit, come and go in the blink of an eye. Ulf struggled with this human dilemma because his painful emotions had no place to hide. They were in stark contrast to his strong desire to be loving and peaceful. In a strange way, this magnified contrast simplified his repeated choice to choose love. (He was more skillful at doing this than I am.)

We have all experienced loss throughout our lives. It can be a loved one, body or brain function, or non-physical things such as lost hope or unfulfilled dreams. Any thought of loss confirms our sense of being incomplete. It is an inevitable part of the uncertainty and impermanence of this existence. To the extent that we recognize change as the creative process allowing for growth, we can avoid the pain and suffering that comes from the fear and resistance to what is. We cannot control what is occurring at any moment in our life, but we can choose how we perceive and respond to it. The awareness of this ability can change our experience to one of love and peace instead of fear and loss. Love says we are complete and whole. That philosophy was the core of my journey with Ulf. I'm reminded how much Ulf taught me about being in the present moment. As I peel away the layers of my ego's protection system, I am again becoming aware of the energy that flows through my body, facilitating a more expansive and loving experience in which there is no loss.

Today I listened again to one of Ulf's recordings. In a soft, gentle voice, Ulf says:

> *"I've got something with the most wonderful person that has ever been. I can feel it. I'm so grateful you are my wife. You are a very fine person, someone I believe in and who's done wonderful things for me. You've helped a lot of other people. You are a valuable individual. One thing we have—let me take your hand—we love each other. And there is an energy that comes from that. You and I truly love each other and we show it many times."*

That is Love speaking yet once again

7. Behind the Clouds

*T*he mist that drifts in over the valley as I peer out the window is somehow reaching inside me and revealing lessons for me to learn. Grief was expected and the added books on my shelf clearly indicate my desire to learn more about this new experience. I have witnessed some of the stages, such as invisible stress manifesting physically in the body, and the multitude of unexpected emotions.

What surprises me is how the experience of losing the presence of someone very close and dear has uncorked what has become stale wine representing a lifetime of unwept tears. It is as if I have spent my life preparing a feast that is hidden somewhere in the clouds of my forgetfulness. How tidy is that! This invisible "feast" manifests itself in all kinds of emotions—apathy, grief, fear, guilt, anger, etc. This "feast" becomes the "food" of our psyche. Some call it the ego; others call it the "pain body" and some call it our sub-conscious mind. However, until we realize that this misguided energy has no sustenance, we cannot release our attachment to it. To ignore it delays the opportunity to stop recycling the past, which is a part of our human conditioning.

In case you haven't noticed, I am using words and "stream of consciousness thinking" to grapple with this not unexpected pain. It brings comfort to me. Writing like this opens me up to the energy Ulf often spoke about—energy that came through him and that he shared with others. Like Ulf, I am sharing my energy through these words.

Grief is not an emotion I have encountered much in my life. It probably comes in many guises that are not easily identifiable as grief. It often takes the catalyst of a jarring emotional experience to let the genie out of the bottle and become aware that we have been nibbling on the same feast all our life. What we are not aware of is the fact that this "feast," which has been stored in our minds, has decayed and is indigestible. We have isolated this emotional feast from the creative cycle, making it stagnant. We often feel the preponderance of this trapped energy and reach in the medicine cabinet for relief.

Initiating the process of freeing this energy seems difficult because we have identified with what we have created. Because it somehow defines us, we keep resuscitating these emotions with the many stories of our life. If we take an honest look at what we have been trying to preserve, and discard it into the garbage, will we starve to death? We probably think so.

All of these emotions and subsequent stories supporting them are spawned in the feeding ground of our fear. The *Course* says there are really only two emotions: Love and Fear. We have used our imagination to create many seemingly different delicacies to disguise fear. We have done the same thing with what we think of as "love."

Often we have used the word "love" to mask our fear of abandonment. These interpretations occur in our dualistic reality where everything has an opposite. Becoming free of our decaying symbols of fear whenever they arise, we experience Love, which has no opposite.

Peering into the cloud of forgetfulness is not for the timid of heart. The desire for peace is the beginning of transforming this toxic waste containing the ingredients of fear into a nurturing abundance of energy we can truthfully call Love. We can do this with simple awareness. When one of our "delicacies" enters our consciousness, ready for consumption, we can recognize it as the imprisoned teardrops of our past, and allow them to fall as raindrops from the clouds. Each time we do this, moment by moment, the cloud vaporizes and those tears become part of the cycle of life again.

Ulf has provided me with this incredible opportunity to transform my clouds to raindrops of love instead of tears from the past. Ulf, I'm so grateful to you for being that gentle, yet persistent catalyst for me to continue learning from our experience. I have a sense we may even still be sharing the same classroom.

8. The Light of Love

As I ponder the ideas of peeking behind the clouds, exploring holographic universes, staying in the present moment, I realize that every thought is a point of view, even those hidden behind the clouds. We can see ourselves as a little dot or part of the whole of whatever universe we think we inhabit. We place judgments on different emotions—happy, sad, angry, depressed, and jubilant—and identify them as "good" and "bad." Unraveling all this can appear to be very complicated, creating more confusion. We try to capture and hang on to the good feelings and experiences, only to have them shift to a negative experience. How unreliable is that! We think we have failed, yet once again, to "get it."

One of the first lessons in the Workbook section of the *Course* addresses this. "These thoughts do not mean anything.... begin by noting the thoughts that cross your mind.... You will find, if you train yourself to look at your thoughts, that they represent such a mixture that, in a sense, none of them can be called "good" or "bad.".... None of them represents your real thoughts, which are being covered up by them."

Living in the absence of the busy distraction of meaningless thoughts can have its rewards as suggested by this lesson in the *Course*: "I feel the Love of God within me now. There is a light in the world you cannot perceive." "Yet you have eyes to see it. It is there for you to look upon. It was not placed in you to be kept hidden from your sight. To feel the love of God within you is to see the world anew, shining in innocence...."

In listening to Ulf speak of love with such simplicity and innocence it is very evident that he allowed the light to shine through his thoughts. He also had the strong urge to share that energy he called love or God with others, in a very gentle manner. This does not mean he avoided negative thoughts. They just did not define him. As I allow myself to experience thoughts without judgment and just sit in awareness of what is in the moment, it does bring a sense of peace to me. Nothing dramatic. As the shadow thoughts slowly cease to attract my attention, I can better observe the light reflected in my life.

As I noted earlier, there was a full moon when Ulf left. On the third moon anniversary, I took the photos that to my surprise included a heart shaped moon. On this night of the sixth moon, I took photos as the moon drifted behind a thin layer of clouds. This lovely light is always shining behind our thin layer of thoughts. My journey now, without Ulf in my world, is one of seeing that light, unobstructed by my fearful thoughts, shining in Love.

EPILOGUE
Opening to Love

*T*he awareness of seeing things differently is what Ulf experienced for several years as his "thinking" brain gave way to other possibilities. I now view Ulf as an explorer who forged a new trail even as the very fabric of how he perceived himself was peeling away. He once told our friend Whit, "I am not the person I used to be." The loss of how we have identified ourselves, whether through change of external circumstances or physically determined causes, is very frightening. Ulf was frustrated and there were times when he would express that frustration. He was able to open to that part of his self that we cover with mental activity. His opening to his Spirit is what I am writing about.

In my experience, the opening to love is evidenced in the dispelling of fear and the quieting of our busy minds. In those moments there is an awareness of connection to something we cannot see, at least not with our eyes. That is also what Ulf experienced. He called it God's energy. That energy was very tangible to him, much more than words or time of day.

Lately, as I ask the question "Where are you Ulf?" and wonder why that is still a mystery, I've become aware of my own emotional ups and downs. Did the fear, worry and constant attention of caring for Ulf close a part of my heart? That's what fear does. It closes our heart. Love opens it. I felt like I had a heart valve that opened and closed depending on the circumstances. Isn't that what we do? Let life determine whether we love or not and whom. That is called projection. I call it "turning the lights out" or "death."

Long ago, we planted seeds that, depending on what we feared or felt safe with, bloomed later in life to mirror back to us what we planted. However, we forgot they were our seeds. The *Course* describes this as the "Obstacles to Peace." So, as I emerge from one cocoon after another (I must be surrounded by invisible butterflies!) I feel more peaceful. There is a sense of expansion as the thoughts and emotions that I felt kept me safe, but closed my heart, are gently viewed as energy that needs to be released and reconnected to my spirit. It is what we are all here to do. This defines our expedition into time and space.

The universe that science is currently exploring has not reached the inner universe of our spirit, which I define as the awareness of who we are and where Ulf's spirit now resides. He has no need of a heart valve that opens and closes. That is what we mortals have installed as part of our survival equipment. We don't need high-powered telescopes to discover our inner world. We just need to befriend and release fear moment by moment and allow the light to flow over the darkness. This is possible *now*. We don't have to wait for science to catch up. How exciting! We can solve the mystery of 'death' by letting the light of love shine through our hearts and dissolve the myth of separation.

* * * * * * * * *

In a strange and compelling way, our last year, which anyone would call the most challenging, has also been one of unparalleled intimacy for Ulf and me. The quiet acceptance of "what is" strips away the external noise of the "what if's." In the nakedness of that realization, our souls are revealed to us in the simplest of ways. Ulf was able to express aspects of himself he had never felt comfortable expressing before. This newly found outlet was exhilarating for him. He sought ways of experiencing this within the context of his limited abilities because, as he said so often, he had to share this energy with others so it would grow larger.

As Ulf settled more into his present moment, I joined him there. It was often a creative venture for both of us captured in a gentle light. Life is never what we expect but we can choose to bring laughter and lightness of being to any situation. Ulf has been an incredible teacher to me and is still teaching me lessons in Love from Spirit.

References

Medical

- Obstructive Sleep Apnea: www.sleepapnea.org
- Dr. Steven Park: *Sleep Interrupted* www.doctorstevenpark.com
- Dr. Mack Jones: *Deadly Sleep*
- Dr. Sung Lee: www.brainwellcenter.com
- Jill Bolte Taylor: *My Stroke of Insight* and TED Presentation video on Youtube

Spiritual/Philosophical

- Foundation for Inner Peace, original publisher of *A Course in Miracles*: www.acim.org; www.acim-archives.org
- Foundation for *A Course in Miracles*: www.facim.org
- Dr. Gerald Jampolsky: *Love Is Letting Go Of Fear*; Center for Attitudinal Healing: www.jerryjampolsky.com and www.ahin-ternational.org
- Eckhart Tolle: *The Power of Now:* www.echarttolletv.com
- Unity Daily Word: www.dailyword.com
- The Sedona Method: www.sedona.com
- Beverly Robbins (Hamilton): *Grains of Sand*: www.amazon.com
- Beverly Hamilton: "How the Step Fell Out of Stepmother," video on YouTube:
- *Peace,* edited by Efrat Sar-Shalom Hanegbie: www.peace-salaam-shalom.com/

Addendum

- Following are specialist in sleep medicine that might be helpful to anyone seeking more information.

- **Steven Y. Park, MD,** Assistant Professor of Otorhinolaryngology (ENT), Albert Einstein College of Medicine; Attending Surgeon, Department of Otorhinolaryngology, Montefiore Medical Center.

- Dr. Park is author of *Sleep Interrupted.* He has a very active website sponsoring free teleseminars and newsletters. His site is listed in the references.

- Here is Dr. Park's response to a *New York Times* article, *When Sleep Apnea Masquerades as Dementia:*

  There are many studies that show how dangerous obstructive sleep apnea is on the brain. One recent study showed lower brain tissue density in areas that control memory, executive function, autonomic control, and breathing. CT studies show a much higher rate of lacunar infarcts in people with untreated obstructive sleep apnea. Others show diminished brain function and metabolism in many critical parts of the brain. A rat study showed that chronic hypoxia leads to beta amyloid plaque buildup in the brain. Numerous studies show that sleep apnea patients have increased levels of inflammatory markers, including CRP, IL2, IL6, TNF, to name just a few. Blood is markedly thicker in sleep apnea—as a result, blood can stagnate in small vessels, leading to microscopic strokes. Areas in the brainstem that control hearing are particularly susceptible to this thickening and clotting.

Obstructive sleep apnea is due to skeletal anatomic narrowing, so it's there long before you develop symptoms. It's also important to note that you don't have to be overweight, male, snore, or have a thick neck to have significant obstructive sleep apnea. Many patients in my practice with sleep apnea are young, thin women that don't snore.

Sleep apnea is such a common problem, even in young people, that if you have early dementia, it just makes sense to screen for obstructive sleep apnea. It's surprising that Alzheimer's researchers and sleep apnea researchers aren't talking to each other. Hypoxia and brain tissue injury is a likely reason for amyloid plaque buildup.

CPAP is the generally recommended first line option, but oral appliances can be used as well for snoring and mild to moderate obstructive sleep apnea. Surgery can also be effective, but only when all the areas of obstruction (nose, palate and tongue) are addressed properly.

It's estimated that 90% of people with obstructive sleep apnea are not diagnosed. Think about all the car accidents and industrial accidents that happen as a result of untreated obstructive sleep apnea. It's also associated with significantly increased risk of hypertension, diabetes, obesity, heart disease, heart attack, and stroke. It's a public health emergency.

From Dr. Parks: Sharecare's list of the "Top 10 Influencers of Online Sleep Discussion," I strongly recommend that you bookmark all these great sites for timely and important information for better sleep and health:

- #1 Dr. Michael J. Breus – TheInsomniaBlog.com
- #2 Brandon Peters, M.D. – http://sleepdisorders.about.com/
- #3 American Academy of Sleep Medicine –http://sleepeducation.blogspot.com/
- #4 Lisa Shives – http://nssleep.com/blog/
- #5 Cleveland Clinic – ClevelandClinic.org
- #6 National Sleep Foundation – SleepFoundation.org
- #7 Deborah Kotz – Boston.com – Daily Dose
- #8 Anahad O'Connor – New York Times – The Well Blog
- #9 Dr. Steven Y. Park – DoctorStevenPark.com
- #10 Dr. Catherine Darley – www.naturalsleepmedicine.net

Dr. Mack Jones, author of the book "Deadly Sleep."

Dr. Jones has been a guest on one of Dr. Park's teleseminars. He wrote this to include here:

I am a retired clinical neurologist and I have Obstructive Sleep Apnea that I discovered in 2001. After a slow, but successful recovery, I wrote "Deadly Sleep," a book about sleep apnea.

Aside from the long list of known complications of Obstructive Sleep Apnea (OSA), i.e. obesity, diabetes, high blood pressure, heart attack, heart failure, cardiac arrest, stroke, depression, ADHD, autism, motor vehicle accidents... and the list goes on, there is mounting evidence that OSA may be the cause of Alzheimer's Disease (AD). Hundreds of apneas while asleep, causing low blood oxygen (hypoxemia) over decades, gradually destroys the brain. If it turns out to be true, then prevention of AD can be done by simply preventing apneas by maintaining an open airway with the use of a continuous positive airway pressure (CPAP) machine. The bottom line: Have a sleep test and if positive for OSA, treat with CPAP and prevent or potentially reverse Pandora's box of diseases, not the least of which may be Alzheimer's Disease.

Dr. Don Curran—Psychiatrist and Sleep Medicine Specialist

The definition of sleep apnea is interrupted breathing during sleep. If we normally breathe approximately 14 breaths per minute while awake, there should be a similar rhythm of breathing while sleeping. In interrupted breathing, there is usually an obstruction of the airway between the nose and the lungs that causes air to not get into the lungs and up to the brain and other organs. If this occurs 10 times a minute or more while sleeping, among many other symptoms, this person will have significant problems with reduced capacity to remember and make decisions. It causes fatigue during the day and often causes auto accidents. It also can result in cognitive disorders such as early type dementia symptoms such as Ulf experienced.

Sleep medicine covers a broad range of sleep disorders that produce many varied symptoms. There is much information on sleep that has not come into the medical mainstream. As a physician, I am interested in researching and properly diagnosing symptoms that may be related to a sleep disorder. Proper treatment can reverse the damaging symptoms and change lives.

Made in the USA
Las Vegas, NV
27 July 2023

75301462R00095